BRANDO

BRANDO

RON OFFEN

HENRY REGNERY COMPANY·CHICAGO

Library of Congress Cataloging in Publication Data

Offen, Ron.
  Brando.

  1. Brando, Marlon.
  PN2287.B68303   791.43'028'0924 [B]   72-11186

For all the secret rebels of my youth,
the Silent Generation, for whom Brando
provided a voice, an alternative, a hope.

Contents

Preface

IN THE wave of recent societal changes—themselves the result of such seemingly incongruous phenomena as economic affluence, a welter of questionable advances in technology, and massive public discontent over such issues as civil rights, environmental destruction, and an unpopular war—it is difficult to imagine the closed, repressive atmosphere that existed in the United States for those of us who felt the first twinges of adolescent idealism and rebellion just after World War II.

We were called the Silent Generation by those observers with a penchant for facile generalizations. No doubt there was a grain of truth in the label, but whether it was fully deserved is open to question, and one can offer an apologia for the lack of militancy by the youth of that era.

It was the time, you may remember, when returning

veterans, welcomed home by a grateful and chauvinistic nation, began to swell college classrooms. They were serious and dedicated students—we referred to them as "grinds"—who doubtless had a stabilizing, even numbing effect on their younger colleagues.

Then, as the horrors of Hiroshima and Nagasaki began to fade from the public consciousness, the Cold War cast an even more chilling shadow on everyone's hopes for world peace. Xenophobia became commonplace; the theory that North Korea had attacked South Korea was readily accepted, as was the resulting "police action" with its waste of lives.

Those who objected to the course our country was taking were highly suspect. It is small wonder that under such conditions an otherwise ineffectual and obscure senator from Wisconsin gained such tremendous power that the term *McCarthyism* became a synonym for demagoguery.

It was a time of witch-hunts, guilt by association, and loyalty oaths. Americans suffered from the effects of an economic recession. The House Un-American Activities Committee was in its heyday—witness the case of the Hollywood Ten. A movie marquee blazing *I Was a Communist for the F.B.I.* wasn't ludicrous in 1951.

Naturally, the temper of the times had a marked effect upon the young. As I remember, the ultimate in sophistication in those days was to be "cool"—uninvolved, detached, uncommitted. Certainly, the young people of the forties and fifties were as aware of society's ills as those of the sixties and early seventies (or twenties and thirties, for that matter). But if the slogan of the sixties was to "turn on, tune in, and drop out," and if the middle-class rebels of the thirties wanted to "live fast, die young, and have a good-looking corpse," the generation between was more concerned with taking it easy, reaching a ripe old age, and obtaining a comprehensive pension plan.

Like the young people of later years, our idols were largely musicians. The difference was that our mentors were of the technically brilliant but politically detached bop school. Charlie "Yardbird" Parker was too wrapped up in his own flight from reality to offer any viable program for action. And although Dizzy Gillespie wore funny hats and became a Moslem, he wasn't leading any protest marches.

The generation that followed ours had at least the tacit approval of the many adults who had been secret rebels twenty or thirty years before, and who thus are partially responsible for the success of the so-called Youth Revolution of the sixties. But in the fifties the generation gap was more impassible. Our parents and teachers offered no support for even a token rebellion. We were told to get a good job (and keep it), get a good education (and use it to improve our economic and social standing), and keep quiet. When I was in college, one of my instructors actually advised me—repeatedly—not to rock the boat by asking controversial questions.

This was the milieu—stagnant, festering—that Marlon Brando entered in the late forties and early fifties. Those of us who lived in the hinterlands did not feel the shock immediately. But we heard about the electrifying brute in Williams's new play, *A Streetcar Named Desire;* we were intrigued by photographs that showed him standing proud and uncompromising in his torn T-shirt and jeans; we heard his inarticulate yet somehow moving delivery parodied by the comedians of the day.

It seemed as though we had been waiting for Brando for a long time. In 1950, when Hollywood finally was able to persuade him to make a movie, *The Men* confirmed what we had been hearing. Brando, as the paraplegic Ken Wilozek, was not just another wounded war vet returning home to struggle with the problems of readjustment. He was an embittered young man who (initially, at least) questioned the value of "fitting in" as well as the other values of what was then a most complacent society.

A year later the general public felt Brando's full force. There had been rumors of obstreperous and unconventional behavior in Hollywood; the gossip columnists had dubbed Brando the Slob, and his rare remarks to the press indicated that the young star was an unregenerate rebel. Still, it was only when he filmed his interpretation of the savage, beer-swilling brother-in-law of the pathetic, phony Blanche du Bois that it all came together.

It is difficult now to ascertain just why Brando's portrayal of Stanley Kowalski in the movie version of *Streetcar* meant so much to us. Certainly, the character was (as Brando repeatedly pointed out) an insensitive, amoral brute. Why, then, was Kowalski such a hero to the conventional as well as to the more-or-less rebellious youth of the time? Was it that even though Kowalski is uncompromising he emerges the winner?

Probably Kowalski's—and Brando's—appeal was a combination of all these factors and more. Pauline Kael, commenting on Brando's stance as a rebel and loner, placed him in the tradition of the movie outlaws and gangsters of the thirties. She noted that if Brando was antisocial, it was because he knew that society was crap. Yes, that was it: here was a young man who recognized and furthermore *acted* upon a premise that we all felt to be valid.

Still, if Brando was a rebel, he was a rebel of his time, "cool," without a cause. In the films that followed

Streetcar Brando stood not *for* things but *against* a great many things. As the hero of *Viva Zapata!*, he fought against a totalitarian regime but was unable to implement a program of action once the revolution had succeeded. Asked what he was rebelling against as the gang leader in *The Wild One*, he could answer only, "What have ya got?" And even as the surreptitious Mark Antony, his only real program was to stand by his own sense of duty and morality and oust the old men who had taken over the state.

Well, we cheered Brando in each of these and subsequent roles. When he received the Academy Award for his electrifying performance in *On the Waterfront*, we could hardly believe it. Didn't Hollywood know what Brando was up to? And even when he assumed the identity of the Little Corporal in *Desiree*, Sky Masterson, a Runyonesque song-and-dance man in *Guys and Dolls*, or an Okinawan houseboy in *Teahouse of the August Moon*, it was somehow a victory. At least he was successfully avoiding the typecasting to which so many stars in the past had succumbed.

In the years that followed we came to admire Brando's lifestyle as well as the roles he mastered: his endless traveling, which seemed to prove his antinationalism; his outsider relationship to Hollywood; and his involvement in such causes as civil rights and the antiwar movement. In addition, there was the phenomenon of his pervasive influence on actors and acting and on the organizational structure of the industry.

The release of *The Godfather*, following almost a decade of work by Brando in less important roles and offbeat films, proved once again that, as Pauline Kael and so many others have commented, Brando is the most accomplished film actor of our time. Many critics have slighted or overlooked the importance of Brando's meticulous and moving interpretation of the aging Don. For some, the portrait of the youngest son, Michael (Al Pacino), was a greater accomplishment. But this overlooks the fact that Don Corleone's commanding presence is felt from the beginning to the end of *The Godfather.* Brando's performance holds the film together, and without him the picture probably would have been just another Mafia extravaganza. At any rate, Brando's magnificent performance in *The Godfather* provided the final impetus for this book.

My task as a biographer was difficult, given the type of man Brando is. He jealously guards his privacy and has a penchant for covering his tracks and giving misleading information. His close friends are singularly loyal; they refuse to discuss him with investigators, even those with the purest of motives. Without the help of such individuals as Len Boscarine, Sidney Hyman, Edith James, Alfred Lutjeans, Walter Oleksy, Charles Palmer, Bruce Trinz, Charles Veley, and the numerous others cited as interviewees in the following pages, my job would have been almost impossible.

Finally, I would like to express my debt to my wife, Rosine, whose help and understanding during the writing of the book contributed the most to its eventual emergence in print.

Ron Offen

BRANDO

1.

Fair-Haired Boy

WHETHER an actor is born or made is a question that has been debated since Thespis mounted the boards in pre-Christian Greece. The life of Marlon Brando, Jr., who made his entrance into the world in Omaha, Nebraska, on April 3, 1924, does little to resolve the argument. As an Aries child, his stars indicated that he was to be a proud man who would lead, pioneer, and generate trends. There are many ways to lead, of course, and Buddy—as young Marlon soon came to be called—undoubtedly was influenced in his choice of a career by his parents, Marlon, Sr., and Dorothy Myers Brando.

The young couple, who were married just after World War I, provided an unusual family atmosphere for their children. Buddy's parents came from old midwestern families, but they were highly mobile, intellectually curious, and slightly unconventional in outlook.

1

Even the name the Brandos passed down to their third child was somewhat unusual. The family name is an Americanization of the French *Brandeau* or *Brandeaux*. The name *Marlon* is evidently also of French origin, belonging to the same family of names as *Marion, Marius,* and *Marlow*—all meaning "dedicated to the Virgin Mary."

Although Buddy may have felt that his name set him apart, his father had encountered no trouble with it. Marlon, Sr., was born in 1895, also in Omaha. A tall, robust man, who some remember as sporting a brush mustache at one time, he was from an established, upper-middle-class family. His solid, conservative background was tempered by a love of travel and a profound interest in the arts.

The father's sales career led the young family to such far-flung places as San Francisco, California, and the Brandos' first daughter, Jocelyn, was born on the West Coast in September, 1919. Perhaps due to his search for prime territory and a good "line," Marlon, Sr., frequently moved his new family around with him.

If restlessness cast Brando's father in the role of a traveling salesman for a good many years, perhaps it was his love of the arts that first attracted him to Dorothy Myers. Dodie or Do, as she was called by her family and friends, was also of old German-American stock that had settled in the Omaha area. Born in Grand Island, Nebraska, around the turn of the century, she exhibited an interest in dramatics at an early age. Those who remember her as a youngster characterize her as a beautiful, quick-witted girl who longed for a life on the stage.

At first, the mobility of the young Brando family precluded a full-fledged career in the theater for Dodie. Then, after the Brandos returned to Omaha to set up housekeeping, a second daughter, Frances, was born in 1922. The house at 3135 Mason Avenue was a very large one in the upper-middle-class Field Club District of the city. Even though Dodie had maids to help her, keeping the small mansion shipshape and being both father and mother to her small daughters while her husband was away on business were full-time jobs.

It was not really until after Buddy was born and the family had settled into a more regular routine that Dodie Brando again began to think about acting. At about this time she joined the Omaha Playhouse, a community theater that staged a number of productions each year. Within a short time she captured roles in such plays as *Pygmalion, Anna Christie,* and *Lilliom.* She made an immediate hit with the local audiences and was rewarded with leads in *He Who Gets Slapped, They Knew What They Wanted, Dear Brutus, The Enchanted Garden,* and many other popular hits.

Dodie was also able to interest her husband in the group. He became quite active in the organization when his busy schedule permitted. In fact, friends from this period recall that he was really a "frustrated actor" who occasionally took bit parts in plays that required a distinguished-looking butler or messenger. Unfortunately, other interests did not allow Marlon, Sr., to develop his talents as fully as his wife did hers.

Dodie's enthusiasm for the theater made her a tireless proselytizer among her friends and acquaintances, and it was not long before she began urging a young man from her native Grand Island to try his hand at acting. The young man had just left the University of Minnesota after deciding against a career in journalism, and within a few months he captured the juvenile lead in Phillip Barry's *You and I.* He stayed under Dodie's tutelage for two years, getting better and better parts, until he left for Des Moines, Iowa, and his professional debut. His name was Henry Fonda.

Meanwhile, young Buddy was growing into a stocky, tow-headed toddler. Family friends remember him as rather impish and adventuresome and recall that his parents were quite "permissive" in dealing with him. A snapshot taken when the boy was about four, which shows Buddy thrusting out his tongue at his two sisters, corroborates the recollections. At any rate, Buddy's mother doted on him, and, as Brando commented later, "She was everything to me." His relationship with his father was a bit more distant. Speaking of his boyhood feelings for Marlon, Sr., Brando once said that his father seemed indifferent to him—that nothing he did seemed to please him. Perhaps Buddy's father, preoccupied with his growing business, felt that the boy was getting enough affection from the female members of the family; certainly, later in life they were close.

His mother was not the only one who delighted in the family's youngest child: Buddy's sisters, who were his constant playmates, were also very fond of him. Frannie, closest to him in age, was Bud's special favorite during these and later years. Jocelyn, often saddled with baby-sitting chores for the two younger children, still managed to tolerate Bud's antics.

Bud's love of high jinks was often expressed in highly competitive behavior. Frannie later remembered that everything was a contest for Bud when he was a young kid—who could jump the farthest, who could eat the most, the fastest, or who could hold his breath the longest. She characterized him as the great challenger for anyone he got involved with.

Around 1930, according to some sources, Marlon, Sr., joined the sales staff of National Carburundum; a change in his territory necessitated a move to a new home in Evanston, Illinois, a suburb of Chicago. They rented a roomy two-story home at 1044 Judson, a shady street lined with expensive old homes. Business was evidently quite good for Marlon, Sr., even in those early Depression days, for Dodie Brando still had a live-in maid to help her with the house.

Evanston neighbors remember Buddy as a blond, stocky youngster with one pant leg rolled up and the other trailing on the ground. That he was a "regular boy" can be seen from the reminiscences of a person who lived across the alley from the Brandos at the time.

"Oh, yes, I remember Buddy Brando," she laughs. "A cute little kid but always up to some kind of devilry. I was constantly chasing his friends and him off our garage roof. He seemed to be the leader of a small band of boys from the neighborhood . . . now what were their names? Anyway, they'd do boyish pranks like throwing stones through our open windows, then run like the dickens when I'd get after them. Not really bad boys, you understand—just, well, boys."

Two of Brando's early neighborhood chums, according to the Brando family's one-time neighbor, were two Greek boys who lived on the next street. One day, just after moving to Evanston, Buddy marched into the front room, where his mother was entertaining guests, with the older of the brothers in tow.

"This is my friend Milton," he supposedly announced to a startled audience, adding with a touch of pride, "He's Greek!"

Milton and his younger brother, Byron, both fondly recall their early friendship with Buddy.

"I was a couple of years older than Bud," Milton remembers, "so he usually ran around with my younger brother. But he was in and out of our home a lot at the time. In fact, Bud and Byron practically lived at each

other's houses. I haven't seen him in years—I dated his
sister Frannie for a while—but I can tell you one thing:
he was a really great guy . . . and a helluva lot of fun.
Whenever he came over, he kept us in stitches."

Byron is able to add a few more details to the
description of young Brando:

"I think Bud is a year older than I am, but we were in
the same grade. As for what he was like, he was a good
deal as he is today—he still contacts me from time to
time when he gets in the area. He's like that, keeps up
with his old friends. The last time he was in, he stopped
and saw my parents one afternoon.

"Anyway, as a boy he was very adventurous, always
up to something. And you know how they usually make
him out a kind of moody loner. Well, that wasn't—
isn't—true at all. He had a great many friends, who all
enjoyed his company. I was really sorry to see him leave
Evanston . . . though we kept in touch and continued
seeing each other somewhat regularly till we were in our
teens. And I'll tell you one thing, he hasn't changed. I
saw him in Hollywood a few years ago and spent a day
with him. He's the same warm, funny guy he was as a
kid."

Neither of the brothers remembers Brando's early
friendship with Wally Cox, another neighbor, who later
became an actor in his own right, playing bit parts in
movies and being featured in the television series "Mr.
Peepers."

Brando's treatment of Cox was not always the most
considerate. Sometimes the scrawny Wally became the
victim of Bud's boyish pranks. One afternoon, for
example, the stronger and older Buddy reportedly tied
Wally to a tree in a vacant lot and then just wandered
away. It wasn't until hours later, when Wally's worried
Mother finally called the police, that Cox was finally freed.

Cox remembers that he and his friends spent a great deal of time pursuing imaginary bad guys or escaping invisible pursuers. They must have huddled around the radio, listening to "Little Orphan Annie," "Jack Armstrong," and "Tom Mix," and rooted through neighbors' garbage cans in search of precious boxtops, Ovaltine seals, and special coupons that would enable them to send away for secret decoder pins, rings that shone in the dark, and hike-o-meters.

One former Evanston teacher recalls both Brando and Cox quite clearly.

"I had the two of them in the fourth grade. And neither one was a boy you'd be likely to forget. Wally was very bright, always had his hand up, always had the right answers. But the Brando boy—well, he was smart enough—it was just that he didn't apply himself. He had trouble with math, as I remember, not because he wouldn't have been able to do the work if he'd applied himself. He just didn't finish his papers . . . kept them stuffed in his desk and forgot to turn them in.

"And he was a bit of a discipline problem. Not really a bad boy, but he talked a lot—in fact, all the time. I remember once I had to send him and a Greek boy out into the hall to stand because they were disrupting the class with their chattering.

"Well, the principal came by and saw them out there and marched them into the room. 'What are these boys doing out in the hall?' he asked. 'They can't be learning much out there.'

"When I told him why they were out there, he took them both home to their parents. It straightened the Greek boy out right away. But it didn't change Bud Brando.

"As I said, though, he was pretty smart. And a real whiz at chess. I remember once he played the superintendent—and darned if he didn't beat him!'"

Brando's second-grade teacher, at the Lincoln School in Evanston, also has a vivid memory of the boy.

"Even at that early age he was very definitely a distinct personality," she states. "Not someone you'd be likely to forget. He was smart, perhaps a bit withdrawn, but he seemed to have a number of friends and be popular with his classmates. If what you read about him in his later life can be believed, or if you can read between the lines, I'd say that as a child he was pretty much what he became as a man."

Perhaps the Evanston teacher who remembers Brando best and with most affection is his fifth-grade teacher. She is recently retired, and there is a lilt to her voice that belies her age. Her humor shines through and is perhaps the reason that she was known as such a popular teacher for so many years. In her description of her former student one can discover the characteristics that Brando as a man was to project so clearly.

"As I picture him now," she begins, "he was a rather small, slender boy with very blond, wavy hair. He always came to school very neatly attired, but within a few minutes he just sort of 'came apart.' I think he tried, though it was evidently just impossible for him to stay neat.

"Of course, he was extremely athletic at the time. And whatever he did, he put his heart and soul into. So it wasn't surprising that his shirt was always out and his hair was always in a jumble."

Commenting that Brando's best subjects were composition, spelling, and math, she continues: "There was no evidence of any 'star' quality in him then. Except that he never hesitated about speaking his mind on any subject. And this he did, regardless of whose opinion he was challenging. I got the impression that he came from a home where speaking one's mind was not only tolerated but more or less expected.

"But what I remember about him the most, and maybe this ties in with his willingness to disagree, is the fact that he was always involved with other people's problems. If two groups of schoolmates were having a to-do about something, Bud was right in there giving his support—usually to the underdog. Not that his position was always the most reasonable or realistic—after all, he was only about ten at the time—but he was never just a passive observer. He wasn't one of those individuals who just pass by incognito; you knew he was around."

As for Bud's overall relationship with his classmates, she concludes, "He wasn't by any means the most popular boy in the class. Yet he wasn't a loner, either. He always seemed to have one group or another of friends around him. And he displayed distinct leadership qualities with his friends, generally being the one the others looked up to for guidance."

Both Brando's teacher and his former chums also have commented on the close relationship between Frannie and her brother at this time. The former teacher remembers how the young girl watched over Buddy carefully, cooling him down when his support of some underdog threatened to get him into serious trouble.

Frannie, a superior, popular student who was a few grades ahead of Buddy at Lincoln, had her own streak of playful unconventionality. Brando related later how he and his sister would run away from home regularly every Sunday afternoon.

He told an interviewer that it wasn't because he and Frannie were unhappy at home; rather, it was strictly for the adventure. They'd start out early in the morning, before anyone was up, with a packed lunch. No one seemed too worried. The pair would be back when they got tired and hungry enough—which was generally around suppertime.

The Brandos remained in the big house on Judson for the next four years. Then, sometime around 1935, they moved to a large apartment on Sheridan Road, a few blocks away from their first Evanston address.

Buddy continued to attend the Lincoln School, still seeing his old friends from Judson Avenue. Summers were spent mainly at the Lee Street beach under the watchful eyes of Jocelyn and Frannie. The boy soon became a strong swimmer.

Perhaps apartment living did not suit the family— though the huge, well-maintained three-flat in which they lived certainly should have provided enough living space. Or perhaps Mr. Brando again felt the urge to head for greener pastures. In any case, around 1937 the Brandos left the Chicago area.

Some seem to remember that the whole family picked up and traveled to California, and there is good reason to believe that this is true. Both Jocelyn and Frannie lived in the Santa Anna, California, home of their maternal grandmother, Elizabeth Myers, at this time. Both girls attended the local high school, and Brando once told an interviewer that he had been expelled from a California school. He also stated, on another occasion, that he failed a Hollywood screen test when he was about twelve.

If Buddy failed to take Hollywood by storm during this stay on the West Coast, his older sister, Jocelyn, was more successful in launching a dramatic career. The 1938 school yearbook from Santa Anna High lists Jocelyn as a graduating senior and notes that she was secretary of the drama club. Further, she captured the lead in two of the student productions—*Seventh Heaven* and *Campus Quaranteen.*

In any case, by 1938 the family was back together in the Midwest, establishing themselves in a very large, old farmhouse on Bradley Road in Libertyville, Illinois—about thirty-five miles northwest of Chicago. The house is still standing and can just be seen from the nearby tollway through a grove of high old elms, maples, and oaks.

The Brandos probably felt that their spacious new home would provide their young son with plenty of growing room. If such was their thinking, however, they had underestimated Buddy's needs.

2.

The Rebel Emerges

Like their son, when Marlon and Dodie Brando did something, they went all the way. Thus, their new home on the outskirts of Libertyville was not merely a country retreat; it was a real farm. They raised a few crops for their own use and also built up quite a menagerie, which included a horse, cow, geese, chickens, rabbits, a Great Dane, and twenty-eight cats.

Buddy added to this list from time to time. He was forever bringing home wounded snakes, birds with broken wings, and buckets of frogs and small fish. He spent quite a bit of time tramping the nearby woods and fields in search of what he thought would be the ideal pet—a baby raccoon.

He never found one; it would be years before this dream became a reality. Meanwhile, Buddy was charged with the care of the family's domestic animals. A family friend later recalled, "One of his main regular chores was milking the cow. He was the only one she would let do it. I guess Bud had the right touch."

He did seem to have a way with animals, an affection for and gentleness with them that was to last him throughout his life. Sometimes this affection ran to extremes, as when his favorite bantam rooster died. Dodie Brando found the dead pet in the chicken house and quickly buried it in the backyard. Somehow, Bud found out where she had laid it to rest and promptly dug it up. When his mother discovered the bird in his room, she again placed it in the ground. But the next day it was in her son's room again when she went in to clean. It wasn't until Bud had received a stern lecture on the health hazards of keeping his erstwhile friend around that he finally gave up. It seemed as though he just couldn't accept the fact of death.

Generosity was another of Bud's characteristics. A railroad trunkline near the Brando's home was often frequented by hobos who were either waiting for a chance to hitch a ride or looking for food or work. When Bud came across them, he always convinced them that his mother would welcome a chance to show her hospitality, and he generally brought them home for a meal.

On one occasion, while hiking along the shores of a small nearby lake, he came across a woman lying in the marsh grass, evidently ill. After talking to her and discovering she had no money, he quickly offered his home as a temporary refuge. Dodie called a hotel in town, had the woman driven there, and arranged to pay the bill.

At about this time, young Brando also began to develop an interest in girls.

Typically, he seemed most attracted to the misfits, young women who, for one reason or another, were not very popular. And many feel that this characteristic carried on well into his manhood.

His grandmother Myers once commented, "Bud always did fall for the cross-eyed girls."

While Bud kept busy with his freshman studies at Libertyville-Fremont High School and his various other interests—tending animals, helping strays, making eyes at puny-looking girls—the rest of the family began to make themselves felt in the community. Mr. Brando within the next few years established the Chemical Feed Products Company with offices in Chicago's financial district on LaSalle Street. As for Dodie Brando, she returned to her interest in the theater.

The arrival of the Brando family must have had quite an impact on the more culturally inclined members of the community. Both Dodie and her husband soon became active participants in the Libertyville Players. Jocelyn, just out of high school but still undecided on a career, joined shortly afterward. And Frannie, entering Libertyville-Fremont as a junior, soon became one of the most promising members of the school's drama club. Though Bud joined the freshman dramatic group, the Curtain Raisers, his efforts were not solely confined to acting.

In 1940 all the Brando family talent was seen on local stages. Dodie directed a cast of ten local women in something called *Oh, Ladies* for the Players. Though the material itself was somewhat conventional, she was able to arouse the curiosity of the area by promising an unusual presentation—one that all her cast members had sworn an oath not to reveal. On opening night the audience was surprised to discover that it had a number of "plants" in its midst. During the course of the evening they stood up and began taking part in the action. Dodie Brando, who kept up with trends in the theater, had borrowed the device from Odet's *Waiting for Lefty*, a play that had been considered *avant garde* a few years earlier.

Prior to this, in 1939, Jocelyn had made her stage debut for the Libertyville Players in *A Bill of Divorcement*. She had captured the lead, and, as the local critic stated, she "almost stole the show." Later, she played the role of Sydney Fairfield in *Wages for Wives* and also directed a series of one-act plays for the group.

Frannie also made her mark in dramatics during this time. During her senior year, aside from being on the staff of the school paper, being a member of the a capella choir, the Latin Club, the Spanish Club, and the Girls Athletic Association, winning an election to become secretary of the Drama Club, and scoring second highest in the school on a general achievement test, she somehow also found time to play the lead in the senior play, *The Bishop Misbehaves*.

Her former teachers remember her as an extremely bright, creative, and engaging girl with a flair for verbal wit. This is supported by her entry in a school limerick contest:

> There once was a husband from Nylon,
> Who seldom was seen with a smile on;
> He explained with a tear,
> My wife's perisphere,
> While I am decidedly trylon.

Bud's career at Libertyville-Fremont High was undistinguished, if not unnoticed. The former principal later stated that Brando's behavior at the school was somewhat irresponsible, that he had little time for extracurricular activities because he spent most of the time after school in the disciplinary study hall.

A notation in the school paper at that time confirms the principal's memory on this count. An article on after-hours study halls singled out one particular boy as leading the freshman class in time spent after school. The writer adds knowingly, "He's even ahead of Bud Brando—and that takes quite a few!"

Still, Bud managed to find time for other, more enjoyable, after-school activities. As we have seen, he belonged to the Curtain Raisers during his freshman year. As a sophomore he was elected vice-president of the dramatics group, and he also made the frosh-soph football squad.

A former teammate recalls playing with Bud on the lightweight team.

"I don't think either one of us weighed more than 110 pounds soaking wet while we were playing. But Bud—I think he was a guard—was really tough competition . . . played his heart out . . . really loved to win. Of course, we never had much of a rooting section— being the lightweight team with our secondhand cast-me-down uniforms and size-twelve shoes—but that didn't make any difference to Bud."

It was probably during this period that Brando suffered a serious injury to one knee. That would account for the fact that he did not play on any of the school's football teams the following year. In any case, he did enough damage to the tendons of one knee to keep him out of the army when he was called for the draft in World War II, and he later said that the knee had been hurt in a football game.

Bud showed an aptitude for the stage even in his years at Libertyville-Fremont. A former classmate, who was in Bud's public speaking class, states that he was at ease before an audience.

"Bud sat next to me in the class," she said. "A neatly

dressed boy, usually with tweed slacks and a white shirt open at the neck, he never struck me as being sloppy. Since he sat next to me, we did quite a bit of joking in class—not that he was the class clown or anything. But he was very funny, had a terrific sense of humor.

"But he was a little aloof for all his good humor. I don't remember if he dated any specific girl. I seem to see him standing around during the school dances in the gym, only getting out on the floor once in a great while.

"In our public speaking class he was one of the outstanding students. When he got into the movies later, people said he was a mumbler. It wasn't true in our class; he enunciated very clearly, and I never had any trouble understanding him. His real specialty was pantomime. I remember one time he did the president, F.D.R. It was really quite good. He played him from a wheelchair, complete with the long cigarette holder. It was really amazing; he had the man's actions down pat."

Brando's former dramatics teacher at Libertyville-Fremont gives his assessment of Bud's early promise as an actor:

"I always liked the boy. He was sensitive and intelligent, and I knew at the time he showed promise in dramatics. He was best at pantomime. And I'll tell you something—he could really abandon himself to a role, lose himself in a part. When he did a piece, he *really* lived it. It seemed like a natural ability, a way he had of being able to shut out the whole world when he was performing."

Commenting on Bud's diction, his teacher said, "Oh, he didn't pay as much attention to his speech as he might have. But this wasn't any serious problem. Perhaps it was caused by a reluctance to appear affected. You see, one of the things I remember most about him as a personality was his distaste of any kind of sham. He just couldn't abide it."

Some former classmates remember seeing Bud in some of the school's dramatic productions; others state that he never appeared on the school stage. The dramatics teacher clarifies this point:

"No, I never did get around to using him in any of the school plays. As I said, he had the ability, but then he was only in the school for the first part of his high school career. And we just didn't use freshmen or sophomores in the junior or senior plays."

Nevertheless, Bud did grace the school boards on at least one occasion, according to back issues of the school paper. At the beginning of Bud's third year, the paper reviewed a "junior assembly."

Probably the most outstanding of the stellar attractions—outstanding especially in quality and quantity of performance—were Bud Brando and Bob Hoskins. Mr. Hoskins revealed himself as a budding Alec Templeton with several fetching one-finger renditions of popular and classical pieces. Later in the program the two sang "Blueberry Hill" with Mr. Brando drawing much applause for a clear soprano obligato.

That kind of horseplay characterized what was to become a lifelong friendship between Brando and Bob Hoskins. They palled around together, double dated, and shared a mutual interest in music. Hoskins, a member of a large, influential, and well-off Libertyville family, began taking trombone lessons at about this time, and Bud talked his parents into buying him a set of drums. Together they planned to start a dance band.

A former friend of the Brando family once commented on the effect of Bud's drums on the household:

"My God, those drums! I guess young Brando was about sixteen at the time. Anyway, anytime you stopped in at the house you were 'treated' to a drum solo—whether you wanted it or not."

Evidently the budding Krupa wasn't too bad. Bud's former drum teacher once told a mutual friend, "The kid's got real talent. It wouldn't have surprised me if he'd gone on to make a real name for himself in the music world."

Ultimately, the lessons did pay off—in a way. For a short time Bud reportedly played a gig at the Green Cockatoo, a local roadhouse.

Bud's association with Hoskins did not always produce such positive results. A former friend of both states that the two were a "bit squirrelly" in those years. "I never could figure out if it was Brando who turned Hoskins on, or the other way around. But both of them were cut-ups with a little left rudder."

Remembering one particular escapade, the man continues: "A few years later, when Hoskins was home on leave from the army, the two of them went up to Wisconsin on a camping trip. They stayed until all their money was gone, then started hitchhiking home. Hoskins was wearing his army uniform, but the rides weren't coming fast enough to suit them. So Brando got hold of some wide adhesive tape and put a big 'P.O.W.' on the back of his T-shirt. When a motorist stopped to ask what was going on, Hoskins told him that Brando was an escaped prisoner of war that he was returning to Fort Sheridan—a few miles from Libertyville—and that he had to get him back to the stockade as soon as possible. The guy went way out of his way to dump them at the gate of the army camp. Meanwhile, all the way back, Brando kept muttering in guttural tones that were supposed to sound like German."

The pranks of Brando and Hoskins didn't always go undetected. At school they were usually caught, and their punishment was an after-school study hall, or "three-fifteen."

Bud's growing restlessness and unruliness were not entirely due to his friendship with Hoskins, of course. Something seemed to be happening to Bud during his middle years of high school. To some he appeared fun-loving and blithe; others noticed a growing aloofness and moodiness, which often found expression in thinly disguised hostility to figures of authority.

The real causes of the young man's increasing rebelliousness are difficult to assess. Typical adolescent idealism and discontent may have had something to do with the change in Bud's personality. Perhaps the threat of an impending war had its effect. Perhaps the causes were closer to home. Bud had always been on very good terms with his mother. Her quick, challenging mind, her love of culture, and her talent for the theater made her an easy person to idealize.

But there was another, darker side to Dodie Brando's personality. It was known in the small, conservative community that she drank.

It is difficult to discover when Dodie's drinking first became a problem. In one of his rare revelations about his personal life, given to an interviewer years later, Brando admitted that after the family moved to Libertyville, his mother's problem became more acute. He stated that he would sometimes come home from school to find the house empty. He would sit with a gnawing feeling in his stomach, waiting for the inevitable phone call from some bartender in the area, who would tell him that his mother would have to be picked up.

Whatever the reasons, Bud's behavior in school finally became so unruly that he was expelled shortly after the beginning of his junior year. Marlon, Sr., evidently alarmed by his son's expulsion from school and determined to nip the discipline problem in the bud, resolved on a rather drastic measure. In short order, Bud was shipped to Faribault, Minnesota, where he was enrolled at the Shattuck Military Academy.

The experience was to be a bitter one for the rebellious young man. For his father, Shattuck proved to be a waste of good money—the school's strict discipline and rigid scheduling simply could not make his son conform.

According to Brando, he tried to be a "good soldier" at first. He went through the paces, kept a spotless uniform, polished his shoes till they shone like mirrors, answered his superior officers and teachers with a crisp, "Yes, sir" or "No, sir," and put up with the ego-breaking hazing that a newcomer had to undergo.

He even appeared in the school's dramatic productions. In one play he was cast in the role of a corpse on a gallows at midnight. In another he was an explorer in an Egyptian tomb. Neither role could have excited much response from his teachers and schoolmates. The parts were small, and he was barely visible in the dim stage light of the two productions.

Eventually, it was most likely the boy's love of pranks and hatred of regimentation that overcame his desire to make a go of the military life. Brando later said that one of the things that drove him crazy was a tower bell. It gonged constantly throughout the day, announcing reveille, class changes, inspections, and mealtimes. Before long, Brando seemed to become obsessed with its reverberating tones, and finally he couldn't stand to hear its pealing one more time. Early one morning, he stole up to the tower, detached the huge bell, and proceeded to bury it in a field off campus. Unfortunately, this provided only temporary relief from the school's assault on his eardrums. Utilizing the public address system, the authorities soon began broadcasting the blare of a bugle to alert their charges to the duties of the day.

The farce of trying to turn Brando into a soldier came to an end in his senior year. Some remember that Bud's expulsion followed a series of minor pranks that culminated in his emptying a chamber pot from his bedroom window onto a superior officer's head. Brando later told a different story, advising that he had a great plan on how he would set off a bomb at the door of one of the teachers' bedrooms. He made a black-powder bomb in the chemistry lab, then used a bottle of Lucky Tiger hair lotion for a wick. He figured that if he poured the hair lotion on the floor leading up to the bomb, he could light it and be safely out of sight in his room when it went off.

Well, the idea worked in principle, at least. The explosion went off while he was tucked neatly in his bed. What he hadn't figured on was the fact that as the hair lotion burned its way to the charge, it left an indelible burn-mark on the floor. It took the school authorities about two seconds to figure out who'd done the dastardly deed.

Naturally, Brando was a hero to his classmates—a nutty hero, but one who had their admiration and sympathy. His fellow seniors even went so far as to circulate a petition on his behalf, hoping to persuade the authorities to give him the right to graduate. It didn't do any good. The "Mad Bomber of Shattuck" was shipped home and admonished not to come back.

When Bud returned to Libertyville, it was already too

late in the term to enroll in another school. He didn't seem too interested in anything.

Brando tried his hand at several things in the months that followed. For a while he was an usher at the Liberty, the local movie house; then he worked part time as a handyman. In the summer of 1943 he landed a job with a local contractor, laying drain tile in swampy farm fields in the area. It was backbreaking labor, but by this time he had begun to fill out and develop an athletic, muscular build. If he did not care for the tedium of digging trenches and laying tile, he probably enjoyed testing his body and the feeling of healthy exhaustion that followed each work day.

He read a great deal, brooded quite a bit, and astounded his parents one day when he announced that he was thinking of becoming a minister. The family, never overly religious, probably didn't take the idea seriously.

When the fall term of 1943 approached and Bud had made no move toward returning to school, the Brandos probably began to worry. Their son seemed uninterested in continuing his formal education; he supposedly maintained that he could learn just as much on his own. The Brandos had only to talk with Bud's teachers and to look at the books he was reading to know that he had a superior mind. Didn't he realize that to get ahead, he would have to go through the paces of an academic training? Without even a high school diploma, his prospects would be limited.

Bud's parents finally decided that perhaps their son needed a change of scene. Dodie, who was planning to take Jocelyn and Frannie to New York, had heard of the New School for Social Research, which she thought might suit her son. He didn't need a high school diploma to enter, and the school's curriculum might just be different enough to tempt him.

But when the mother and daughters left Libertyville, Bud remained behind—at least for the time being. Dodie had her hands full getting her two girls established.

Jocelyn, by this time, had already completed one year at Lake Forest College, at the time a more-or-less upper-class finishing school near Libertyville. She soon seemed to realize that she was not cut out for the academic life or the rah-rah of the sorority-fraternity social whirl that the school offered. She wanted to act and so continued to work with the Libertyville Players and other nearby community theater groups.

Frannie's goal when she graduated from high school had been to "be an interesting person." She had spent a year at the University of California at Los Angeles, where her fellow students jokingly referred to her as the Bug (because of the huge, round glasses she sported) and where she developed a consuming interest in art.

When the Brando women arrived in New York, Dodie quickly found a small apartment for her girls, enrolled Frannie in the Art Students' League, and then went around to see some of her old friends in the theater. Through them, Jocelyn was able to get a few auditions and eventually land some small roles. Later, Dodie's friendship with Henry Fonda probably helped Jocelyn obtain a good part in *Mr. Roberts*. Her work in this long-running hit won her critical praise, and she continued her career on Broadway in such plays as *Desire Under the Elms* and *Golden State*.

Shortly after his sisters had settled down, Bud came to New York to live with them. He worked at several part-time and temporary jobs at first, feeling his way around. One of these was elevator operator at Best's department store in Manhattan, but he lasted only a few weeks. It seems that calling out "Third floor—women's lingerie" hundreds of times a day made him feel uncomfortable.

After getting established in the city, he began to take courses at the New School—"for the lack of anything better to do," as he commented later. At first he studied any subject that struck his fancy: psychology, art, history, conversational French, Far Eastern philosophy—even handwriting analysis. Later, he became a theater major and enrolled in the school's Drama Workshop.

The Drama Workshop, under the brilliant leadership of Stella Adler and Erwin Piscator, was to become (along with the Actors' Studio of Lee Strasberg) an important training ground for some of the biggest stars of stage and screen in the decades to follow. Stella Adler was a member of an old, established theatrical family (her brothers were Luther and Jay); Piscator had been involved in the Berlin theater of the twenties. Adler and Piscator, along with Strasberg, were the leading exponents of the Method school of acting in America.

This acting style was still relatively new in 1943 when Brando first came across it in Stella Adler's classes. It had been introduced in the United States about two years before by Richard Boleslavsky and Maria Ouspenskaya, both of whom had studied with the legendary Stanislavsky in their native Russia. Method acting requires a player to "get inside" a character. Using such terms as *emotional memory* and *private moment,* it stresses that the actor must draw on personal emotional resources to make a character vital, believable, and three dimensional.

The Method approach to acting immediately appealed to Brando. Perhaps for the first time in his life he began working really hard at something. He seemed to find an outlet in his acting classes, and he utilized them well.

Stella Adler was quick to recognize the ability of her new pupil, the power he could project to an audience. After only a few weeks she was telling people, "My puppy-thing is going to be the best young actor in America within a year." Her enthusiasm was shared by Piscator, who predicted a "brilliant future" for Brando.

The young actor's first chance to show what he could do came in the summer of 1944. He was hired by a summer stock company in Sayville, New York, for walk-ons and other minor parts. The resident director and his fellow actors found Brando hard working and dependable, for the most part.

As a messenger in the third act of a modern melodrama, Brando garnered his first critical notice. Unfortunately, it was not the kind of clipping one could send home to the family. On the opening night, when a local critic was present, Brando almost flubbed a crucial line. Later, perusing the critic's review, Brando must have felt a sinking sensation in his stomach as he read, "The young man delivering a message about a disaster in the final act nearly created another one."

In this same period, just after coming to New York, Brando was to renew a friendship from his Evanston days. Wally Cox was studying industrial arts at New York University. It was lonely in the big city and difficult to find dates. So when Cox heard that the Brando girls were in town, he trotted over to their apartment.

When Wally heard that Bud was also in town, the two soon became as inseparable as they had been almost ten years before. Cox had a variety of off-beat interests, from silversmithing to model trains to playing the recorder. In addition to acting, Brando was studying Zen Buddhism, the bongos, and yoga. Together they made quite a pair.

Before long, Brando and Cox decided to set up their own apartment. One of the liveliest New York neighborhoods at the time was on West Fifty-Seventh Street. There, such jazz greats as Coleman Hawkins, Dizzy Gillespie, and Erroll Garner were featured in small, smoky clubs—the Three Deuces, the Onyx, and the Spotlight, to name but a few. It was the perfect milieu for those who played bongo-recorder duets all night and opened their doors at any hour to people in search of conversation or a place to flop.

People who knew Cox and Brando in those days remember their "pad" as a Grand Central Station for aspiring actors, assorted intellectuals, and local characters. In one section of the cramped living quarters Cox set up his model trains; in another, his silversmithing equipment. Under a jumble of soiled clothing one might find Brando's Cuban bongos, while hanging from the wall were his fencing foils. In the middle of the room were some caked paint buckets, left over from an ambitious attempt to redecorate the flat. Shelley Winters, an occasional guest, remembers what took place: "I think they got one wall done, then gave up. They just left the buckets of paint in the middle of the floor with the brushes stuck in them."

The action was fast and furious. While a homeless friend napped on the floor, the two hosts might be playing a duet or amusing each other with imitations. Cox's specialty was juvenile delinquents (which he later perfected for his famous "Dufo, What a Crazy Guy" routine). Brando went in for less obvious subjects, such as a rock, or a worm emerging from a cookie.

Commenting on his roommate's ability to get inside almost any subject, Cox once said, "Marlon's one of the best 'diggers' alive. He can dig anything, imitate anything. And what a comic—he can bring out such laughter that it can give you pains in your stomach."

A cardboard sign that Brando had scrawled in crayon and hung on a wall set the tone for the apartment: "You ain't living if you don't know it." Everyone who passed through the two friends' door knew that a great deal of living was going on inside. In the middle of the night Brando might suggest that they all go out for sodas or milkshakes. (He was a strict teetotaler at the time, and it was understood by those who dropped in that liquor was not part of the scene.) At other times, to liven things up, they would fill paper bags with water and drop them on the heads of people below as they staggered out of the jazz joints and into the predawn air.

But Brando didn't always join in the fun. An acquaintance who sometimes sought refuge in the apartment recalled that the young actor had his darker moments: "He was a brooder. He seemed to have some secret place he'd withdraw to, to worry about himself and life."

Another acquaintance stated that one couldn't get Brando involved in a conversation with more than one person at a time. He evidently couldn't handle it. With one person, reportedly, he'd be interested and attentive—and, well, sweet. Brando, the acquaintance said, was not interested in using anyone. If he thought someone could do him a favor as far as his career was concerned, he'd avoid him.

The same attitude seemed to characterize Brando's relationships with women at the time. The young actor wasn't attracted to show-biz types. Usually, he dated young secretaries, college students, or girls who weren't aware of his aspirations as an actor.

And what of those aspirations? Did he want to spend his life tearing himself apart on the stage for an audience? He must have known that he had a special talent. Stella Adler had confided to a friend, "Marlon was a natural—never really had to learn acting. From the beginning he was a universal actor. He had the potential for any role because nothing seemed foreign to him. In addition, he's got an incredible range of emotions—plus looks, voice, and power of presence."

If his teacher's words of commendation got back to him, Brando still made no move to crystallize his acting career. Where was he going? And did he really want to make the trip?

3.

Stel-la!

I t is difficult to imagine the impact that twenty-three-year-old Marlon Brando had on the audience that filled Broadway's Barrymore Theatre on December 3, 1947—opening night of Tennessee Williams's *A Streetcar Named Desire.* The power and energy he brought to the role of Stanley Kowalski, the brutal, beer-swilling antihero, stunned the audience, left them wondering what had hit them. This was a kind of acting that had never been seen before on the American stage. Like Bernhardt in *Camille* or Lotte Lenya in *The Threepenny Opera,* Brando in *Streetcar* was a once-in-a-generation experience.

Critical acclaim for the play in general and Brando in particular came almost immediately. One critic wrote the next day, "It was awful and at the same time sublime. Most people see that kind of performance only once in a lifetime."

Brooks Atkinson praised the script and direction, the performances of all the principals, and wrote that Brando's characterization of the "braggart, sullen, caustic brother-in-law" had galvanized the entire production.

Fellow actors also were quick to realize that a giant had emerged in their midst. Walter Matthau later admitted that he had seen 186 performances of the play. William Redfield, the actor who played *Hamlet* on Broadway and went on to a career in the movies, wrote later in his *Letters from an Actor,* "His [Brando's] stage Kowalski generated true mystery and overwhelming excitement." Calling Brando the "God Priapus of modern American playing," Redfield maintained that a whole generation of actors saw him "not only as an actor but also as an artistic, spiritual, and specifically American leader."

The play and production were to win numerous awards the following year. Williams received the Pulitzer Prize for the script. The Broadway production captured the coveted New York Drama Critics Award and the Donaldson Award by virtually unanimous acclaim.

Finally, as his Kowalski portrayal gained wider attention, comics began to parody Brando's style and delivery. Before long, the image of an inarticulate half-animal in torn T-shirt screaming "Stel-la!" became public property.

Once the initial shock of Brando's performance had worn off, people began to ask who this young dynamo was, where had he come from, and why had he never been noticed before?

To answer those questions one must go back to the fall of 1944. An agent seeing Brando's work for the stock company in Sayville, New York, liked his acting and arranged an audition for *I Remember Mama.* When

Brando read for director John Van Druten, who had adapted the play from the Kathryn Forbes autobiography, *Mama's Bank Account,* he captured the role of Nels.

I Remember Mama was a big break for Brando. In the cast were such established stars as Joan Teizel, Mady Christians, Richard Bishop, and Oscar Homolka. Van Druten was fresh from the success of his play *The Voice of the Turtle.* As a testimony to the promise the enterprise showed, Richard Rogers and Oscar Hammerstein II momentarily dropped their pencil and piano and decided to produce their first nonmusical offering.

The period piece about Norwegian-American life in turn-of-the-century San Francisco was an immediate success. Really less a play than a series of scenes in which the intrepid matriarch guides her family through one near-disaster after another, it received six curtain calls when it opened at the Music Box in October, 1944.

Though the *New York Times* critic, Lewis Nichols, didn't mention Brando's portrayal of the fifteen-year-old Nels, he did note that Van Druten had assembled "some wonderful actors to play the various parts." But others mentioned the young actor briefly, calling Brando's work "memorable" and "noteworthy." All predicted a long run for the middle-brow comedy—a forecast that proved to be accurate. *I Remember Mama* broke attendance records at the theater and continued to be the most popular play until 1946, when it finally closed in New York and went on the road.

Brando did not remain with the show for its entire run of 713 performances. After playing the role for almost a year, he seemed to get restless. Life with Cox may have been as exciting as ever, but perhaps it was becoming a bit nerve-racking. Brando seemed to need time alone to chart his future, to mull over the question of whether he wanted to devote the rest of his life to the stage.

For his retreat he chose the city that had attracted American artists, writers, and intellectuals a generation before. Paris, the City of Lights, was still considered by the young people of the mid-forties to be the cultural center of the world. So, with the money he had saved from his work on Broadway and probably with no particular plans, the actor set sail to test his conversational French.

In Paris, Brando seems to have done little except wander about by himself, frequenting the sidewalk cafés and attempting to engage passing strangers in conversation. If such was the case, Brando's first visit to Paris was typical of other subsequent trips to the French capital. Always he used it as a place of refuge; the city offered him anonymity and a milieu that didn't interfere with his long, long thoughts.

By the time Brando's money ran out, he was seemingly more at peace with himself though still undecided about his future. Back in New York, he rejoined Cox and the group of actors and intellectuals that somehow looked to him for leadership. Cox later said, "He's a creative philosopher, a very deep thinker. He was a liberating force to his friends."

After kicking around for a few months, Brando decided to give acting another whirl. The play he auditioned for was destined to become one of the most disastrous productions he was ever associated with—and also one of the most important for his future career.

Broadway was in the doldrums at the time, at least so far as serious plays were concerned. Older playwrights, for the most part, were resting on their laurels; and a new generation of young dramatists had yet to emerge.

Into this atmosphere Maxwell Anderson brought his *Truckline Café*. Featuring a cast of thirty-five and a number of scene changes, it promised to be an expensive production. As usual, Anderson was attempting to get a message across—in this instance the effects of World War II on those who went off to the battlefields and on those who were left behind. The show had a promising cast under the direction of Elia Kazan and a young actor from the Playwright's Company who was getting more and more attention.

Unfortunately, the critics of the major New York papers panned the play unanimously. Lewis Nichols of the *New York Times* felt that Anderson must have written it with his left hand by the dark of the moon. Nichols wrote, "A large cast finds itself entangled in short incidents without great meaning and saying lines which now and then dip backward to bathos."

As for Brando, Nichols noted only, "Ann Shepherd and Marlon Brando are the couple which ends as victim and murderer." But others thought Brando's interpretation of the returning army sergeant who suspects his wife of carrying on with his friend was "quite effective."

The critical reaction to the work sparked a bitter controversy in theatrical circles. A few days after the opening, a large, three-column display ad paid for by co-producers Kazan and Clurman appeared on the amusement page of the *New York Times*. In it the two men declared their belief in the play but announced that due to the lack of audience response they would be forced to close the following week. Attacking all the leading New York critics, they charged that a small circle of irresponsible people had a stranglehold on the American theater. Without the critics' approval, they said, audiences would not patronize a production; without an audience, there was no way for producers to offer new theater in view of rising costs on Broadway.

The attack had little effect. A few people wrote letters to the *New York Times* supporting Kazan and Clurman and praising the play. But all the same, *Truckline Café* closed on the announced date.

The importance of the play for Brando was that it gave him the opportunity to work with Kazan. Though the premature closing of the play cut short the development of a close relationship, Kazan had been impressed by the young actor and would remember him favorably later. In addition, it was during the course of the doomed production that Brando met Karl Malden. The former steel worker from Gary, Indiana, with his down-to-earth midwestern outlook, and the aspiring actor from Libertyville, Illinois, became good friends.

Whether or not the critics were bowled over by young Brando's work, other influential people in the theater were taking note. Typical of these was the mother of Stella Adler, an octogenarian veteran of the stage who attended the opening night performance of *Truckline*. Coming backstage with her daughter to talk to Brando after the performance, Stella's mother leaned on her gold-headed cane, fixed him with a penetrating stare, and said, "This is an actor—and if this actor doesn't rise to his potential, I shall return from my grave to haunt him!"

Unfortunately, he did not have the same effect on all of the prominent theater people he encountered. About this time, Brando auditioned for Alfred Lunt and Lynn Fontaine, who were casting for their production of *Mistress Mine*. When Brando's turn came, they handed him a script and asked him to read.

He couldn't make out the small type on the dimly lit stage. (Brando's brownish-gray eyes were becoming increasingly nearsighted. He tried wearing glasses from time to time, but he kept losing them. Finally, he just gave up and struggled along without them.)

He told the waiting Lunt that he was having difficulties because he had lost his glasses.

"Well, just say something, recite anything you know from memory," the impatient Lunt called out.

Brando fidgetted for a moment, then struck a heroic pose.

"Hickory, dickory dock," he declaimed. "The mouse ran up the clock . . . "

When he was finished, they expressed their thanks and gave him the old "don't call us, we'll call you" routine.

Brando had better luck when he read for Katharine Cornell early in 1946. The veteran actress was planning a revival of Shaw's *Candida.* She had become associated with the play in 1942, when she played the title role in the revival of that year. She was immediately impressed with Brando and cast him as the poet, Marchbanks. It was a sizable and important role for the young actor. Moreover, his pay was to be a handsome $300 a week.

Brando was probably astounded at receiving the part. The other members of the cast were of the same high caliber as Cornell. Mildred Natwick had been recruited to play Miss Garnett, the brisk, pert secretary. And assuming the role of the bumptious Burgess was Cedric Hardwicke. It promised to be an historic production.

On opening night the critics were not exactly enthralled, but they were impressed. Cornell, Natwick, and Hardwicke carried off the honors. But some felt that the show lacked the fire of Cornell's '42 revival—perhaps a euphemistic way of saying that the actress was getting a bit old for the title role.

The response to Brando was mixed. One critic found his interpretation of the weak, romantic Marchbanks "superb." Another stated, "Though Mr. Brando might not physically fit the role of the frail poet, his reading convinces us of the essential sensitivity of the character." Lewis Nichols noted in the *New York Times:* "The world will always quarrel about Marchbanks and the various interpretations possible thereof. Marlon Brando emphasizes the weakness and banks the fire, the result being a somewhat monstrously intoning poet. His version is not believable since it fails to prove, among other things, why Morell should pay any attention to him."

Evidently, Nichols did not read Shaw's own comments on the character: "He is a strange, shy youth of eighteen, slight, effeminate, with a delicate childish voice and a haunted, tormented expression and shrinking manner that shew [sic] the painful sensitiveness of very swift and acute apprehensiveness in youth. . . . Miserable and irresolute, he does not understand where to stand or what to do."

Cornell and the rest of Brando's fellow cast members paid no attention to adverse critical commentary on the young actor. They knew he was good and told him so. Consequently, it was with some sadness that they heard the news that Brando would be leaving the cast. The show was successful, and an extended road tour was planned. Cornell reportedly tried to talk him out of leaving, but evidently he had made up his mind.

Brando was beginning to exhibit a characteristic that would grow more pronounced as time passed. There was more to life than acting, and Brando began to associate himself with what he probably considered to be worthwhile causes. As we have seen, even in his early boyhood he had aligned himself with underdogs. Following the end of World War II, one of the most widely discussed political issues was the fate of millions of displaced European Jews. Various ways of dealing with the problem were suggested, including the establishment of Israel as an independent Jewish state.

It was against this background that Ben Hecht, the Chicago newsman who had gone to Hollywood to make his fortune, offered his new play *A Flag Is Born.* A militant, emotionally charged piece of theater, it was largely an attack upon the British handling of the Palestine problem. It also criticized the United States and the other major powers for dragging their feet on the Palestine question, and it reproached American Jews for their complacency over the issue.

Just how Brando became connected with the production is a matter of conjecture. Stella Adler probably had a hand in wooing her former student away from *Candida.* Stella's brother Luther was directing the offering. He had gathered some of the top talent in America to present the play. Incidental music was composed by Kurt Weil, Paul Muni headed the cast, and Quentin Reynolds took to the stage as the speaker who tied the action together.

When someone asked Brando why he had left *Candida* for *A Flag Is Born,* he said simply, "I felt I should do something for the cause."

The play had a stormy history both on and off Broadway. The British reacted with understandable hostility and bitterness. The London *Evening Standard* called it the "most virulently anti-British play ever staged in the United States." When Hecht attempted to mail his script to Canada, it was seized by Canadian postal officials and refused entry. A United States senator wrote to Eleanor Roosevelt (as well as to such people as Will Rogers, Jr., and Louis Bromfield, one of the sponsors of the play) asking that she denounce the work as "an appeal to terrorism." In Palestine the play was banned, and the leader of a Hebrew university near Jerusalem decried what he called the militant Zionism in the work.

The scene in the play that evidently alarmed its detractors most was the finale. As David, the young militant Jew, Brando raised a rifle in what appeared to be a call to arms and declared, "The new Jewish voice speaks from out of these guns."

Atkinson, writing in the *New York Times,* found this scene one of the most memorable in the production. He noted, "After scribbling around at random for most of the evening, Mr. Hecht gets around to the main point in the final scene and states it with force and vigor." Although Atkinson didn't mention Brando's performance specifically, another critic found the actor the "bright particular star of the evening."

Despite its stormy history, *Flag* was a tremendously popular play. Proceeds went to the Repatriation Fund, which sought to help displaced Jewish refugees, and it was estimated that almost 50,000 Americans saw the play in New York before it closed four months later to tour the United States.

Brando was seemingly not interested in leaving New York to tour and began looking around for another production. His agent told him of a part in a rather offbeat play. If he could manage to work with a highly neurotic, flamboyant star, it could prove to be a big break for him.

The play was Jean Cocteau's *The Eagle Has Two Heads,* a murky, poetic work that was practically a one-woman show. The star was the irrepressible Tallulah Bankhead.

Brando made his appearance at tryouts and won the male lead. But playing opposite the unpredictable Tallulah was more than either of them could bear. The production was to open in Wilmington, Delaware, then move on to Washington and Boston before opening on Broadway. Early in rehearsals both the principals and the director knew they had made a terrible mistake.

Tallulah had a profound distrust of the new Method actors. Brando's uninhibited behavior almost drove her to distraction. An observer of one of their early rehearsals said that a scene in which Brando, as a revolutionary young poet, chased Bankhead, playing a queen, around a regal bedroom looked like something out of a Keystone comedy.

Later Bankhead admitted, "Brando is terribly talented." She also added, "However, I think he's rather strange." Some years later Tallulah used Brando's name as a bribe when she was hospitalized from the effects of her hard life. She promised a nurse an introduction to the star if the nurse would stay by her bedside till morning.

In any case, by the time the play opened out of town, the German actor Helmut Dantine had replaced Brando. Perhaps it was just as well: the show was universally panned and lasted only twenty-nine performances when it finally reached New York.

By March, 1947, Brando was again in Europe. He stayed mostly in Paris, haunting the Left Bank cafés and talking with the existentialists, who were expounding on the new philosophy of Jean-Paul Sartre. It was on this visit to Paris that Brando met a woman he had long idealized.

In New York intellectual circles one of the most talked-about films was *Les Enfants du Paradis,* which had opened in the mid-forties. Brando had seen the classic a number of times and reportedly had developed a mild obsession about Arletty, the French star who specialized in portraying world-weary, sophisticated

women and who was featured in *Les Enfants* with
Jean-Louis Barrault. Despite the fact that Arletty was
close to fifty at the time, Brando wanted very much to
meet his romantic idol.

Through some mutual friends, an introduction finally
was arranged. The meeting was evidently a disaster.
Brando later called the encounter a mistake and
commented that she was some tough cookie.

After kicking around Paris and Europe for a few
months, Brando returned to New York. Once more he
enrolled in a few classes at the New School. To keep in
shape, he began hanging around Stillman's Gym, sparring with both the up-and-comers and the has-beens. He
also started taking dancing lessons at the Kathryn
Dunham Studio and continued with his fencing lessons.

Though Brando seemed to be engaged in a flurry of
meaningless activity, he was using his experiences to
sharpen his skills as an actor. Wally Cox once said of
him, "He wants to know something about everything.
The things he picks up are an actor's tools." Brando had
prepared himself well. When the 1947 New York season
rolled around, and with it the opportunity that would
launch him into stardom, the actor was ready.

The most promising event of the season was the
opening of a new play by Tennessee Williams. Three
years before, the relatively unknown playwright-poet
had caused an overnight sensation with *The Glass
Menagerie*. It heralded a new voice in the American
theater and marked the introduction of a major talent.
Williams, with his new-found success, had gone to
Mexico to write a new work which he tentatively
entitled *The Poker Party*. But it was as *A Streetcar
Named Desire* that the play became the most talked-
about critical and commercial success that had hit
Broadway in almost a generation.

The play was backed by big money and big talent. Irene Selznick, the daughter of movie mogul Louis B. Mayer, was producing the show. Elia Kazan was to direct. And cast in the principal and supporting roles were Jessica Tandy, Kim Hunter, and Karl Malden.

The only cause for concern was the lack of a male lead. In August, 1947, Irene Selznick announced that John Garfield would play the part of Stanley Kowalski. The role would return the popular movie star to the stage after a long absence and at the same time reunite him with Kazan, with whom he had worked in the thirties in the Group Theatre. Garfield, however, was beginning to have trouble with the House Un-American Activities Committee. Further, after reading the script, he made an evaluation of the Kowalski role that must stand as some kind of milestone in the history of an actor misreading or underestimating a part. In any event, he told Selznick that he didn't want the role of Stanley Kowalski because it was eclipsed by that of the tormented Blanche du Bois.

Dumbfounded, Kazan and Selznick tried to find another experienced, well-known actor who could handle the demanding role. They thought at first of Burt Lancaster. Fortunately for Brando, Lancaster was tied up with movie commitments at the time. Then Irene Selznick brought up Brando's name. She'd seen him in *A Flag Is Born* and had been impressed with the power he'd exhibited. Kazan remembered him from *Truckline Café* and agreed to give him a reading.

As soon as they heard Brando uttering the lines of the play, the producer and director knew that they had found their Kowalski. But by prior agreement, Williams also had to give his approval. They told Brando to rush up to Provincetown, where Williams was staying temporarily, so that the author could give his opinion.

Brando was either too excited or too embarrassed to

mention that he was flat broke and had no means of transportation. He took a subway out of Manhattan and then hitchhiked the rest of the way. He arrived that night, drenched to the skin, in the middle of a storm that had knocked down all of the surrounding power lines. By candlelight, he and Williams read through the entire play. When they finished, the excited Williams tried to contact Kazan. The phone was out of order, and it wasn't until the following morning that Williams was able to tell the director that they indeed had found a Stanley Kowalski.

Streetcar received a great deal of publicity even before it opened. The Sunday supplements of the New York papers ran photo features on the progress of Jo Meilziner's exquisite set, cartoons of the cast members, and comments by Kazan and Williams. Irene Selznick commissioned Thomas Hart Benton, the famous artist of the thirties, to do an oil of a scene from the play.

The play opened to unanimous acclaim, and its fame spread quickly throughout the country and the world. Sir Lawrence Olivier produced and directed a London production, with his wife, Vivien Leigh, in the role of Blanche. Later, Jean Cocteau presented a sexed-up version in Paris, with Arletty as Blanche and nude belly dancers undulating in the background.

If the role of Kowalski was the most auspicious of Brando's career, it was also the one that caused him the most embarrassment and trouble in later years. Probably in his attempt to penetrate the very core of the character, Brando lived the part both offstage and on. As a result, he quickly became characterized as a boorish, inarticulate brute, who was about as sensitive as a chunk of coarse pig iron. And since he was attempting to capture the speech patterns and mannerisms of a Polish-American mechanic, he was soon referred to as the Mumbler by those writers who were lucky enough to interview him.

It evidently made little difference to the reporters of the day that Brando was throwing his whole being into the part. It was much easier for writers to imply that Brando's success was due to the fact that he had been typecast. The actor was forced to fight for years to overcome the Kowalski stereotype.

Commenting on Kowalski's character, Brando told one interviewer that he saw Stanley as a guy who works hard, has lots of flesh, and never really opens his fists—a guy who grips a cup or glass like an animal, wrapping his paw around it and is so muscle-bound he can hardly open his mouth to speak.

To another writer he explained that Kowalski is insensitive, completely without morals, aggressive, unpremeditated, overt, and totally without doubt about himself. In short, the direct antithesis of Brando himself.

Brando's sensitivity and early shyness were borne out by his friends and associates. Kazan said, "Marlon is one of the gentlest—probably *the* gentlest—person I've ever known." Another associate maintained that Brando had once said that if only one person in a crowded room was hostile to him, he had to get out.

Brando's fellow actors were lavish in their praise of his work. Kim Hunter, who played Stella, Kowalski's wife, said, "Those of us who have worked with Marlon are a fan club."

Malden, who later joined his friend in Hollywood, explained Brando's particular genius: "He's so great he makes everyone else look good. He keeps you on your toes, makes you listen, never lets you get used to a certain rhythm."

Jessica Tandy, on the other hand, didn't always care

for the fact that Brando was often different from one performance to the next. She was a product of a different school of acting, and she and Brando disagreed on a number of things. After he had left the show, Brando commented facetiously on their differences: "We don't see eye-to-eye on some things. She believes you should shave and get dressed for a day in the country. Besides, she doesn't like peanut butter."

When asked about her young co-star, Tandy said, "Oh, boy, he's dynamite—everyone in the cast loved him." But she added, "Sometimes we'd also have been happy to knock him on the head. Occasionally he'd just go into a trance on stage. Then I'd find myself playing to thin air."

For the most part, the cast was a happy family, working hard and playing hard together. Brando's favorite form of amusement during midweek rehearsals was boxing with the stagehands. Once afternoon, after the play had been running for quite a few months, he was sparring with a stagehand in the basement to show off the skills he'd been learning at Stillman's Gym. Unfortunately, he didn't see a right cross coming from his opponent; suddenly he felt a numb sensation spreading across the center of his face. Dazed, he raised one hand to his formerly aquiline nose and found it bleeding and flattened. The stagehand, alarmed and realizing that Brando probably wouldn't be able to go on that night, rushed him to a hospital.

After he'd been examined and put to bed to rest until the swelling went down, Brando received a concerned call from Irene Selznick. To her question, he offered a muted rejoinder, and she rushed to his side.

Arriving at the hospital, she found Brando's head practically mummified under swaths of bandages. He had talked a nurse into helping him effect the transformation. Knowing the surest way to win Irene Selznick's sympathy (and thus gain a few days' respite from the play), he played the show-must-go-on gambit to the hilt.

In old trouper fashion he told her he'd go on that night. She would have none of it, insisting that he stay where he was.

Brando remained hospitalized for almost a week, kidding with the nurses, catching up on his reading, taking it easy. When he returned to work, his nose had a very definite bump in it. But Selznick could not admit that her star was flawed in any way. She told people that Marlon was lucky that his nose hadn't been set properly. "He was really too beautiful before," she explained. "The broken nose gives him—I don't know—more sex appeal."

One of Brando's sparring partners at Stillman's Gym, who had to be a bit more careful of his punches after Brando's nose had healed, was former middleweight champion Rocky Graziano. One day the fighter got around to asking Brando what he did for a living. The would-be boxer told him he was in a play on Broadway.

"No kiddin'," said Graziano. "Hey, maybe you could get some tickets for me and my wife?"

The next time he went down to Stillman's, Brando handed a pair of complimentary tickets to the Rock. Wondering how the kid had so much pull, Graziano thanked him and said they'd look for him on stage.

"So we don't miss ya, what act are ya in?" Graziano asked.

Brando replied that he was in all of them.

The former champ and his wife made the trip downtown on the appointed evening, and Graziano almost fell out of his seat when Brando swaggered on stage. "Jesus, that's him!" the fighter exclaimed. "That's the kid I spar with." His wife quieted him down, but he kept whispering throughout the performance, "That's him, that's really him!" Later he admitted that Brando had been so modest about his role in the play that he thought the actor must have had the part of a butler or messenger.

One of the things that seemed to bother Brando after *Streetcar* had been running for more than a year was that his performance was getting flat. He tried every means of breathing new life into his portrayal, even going so far, it has been said, as to get slightly drunk just before the performance.

Of a far more serious nature were the changes Brando began to make in the script. Williams, always a stickler for precision and suspicious of anyone who tampered with his lines, often sat in the audience to see how things were going. One night he noticed that Brando wasn't speaking the words that had been written for him. Upset over the liberties the actor was taking, Williams immediately got in touch with Selznick. The producer was aware of Brando's changes—he had added new business and had cut and altered lines. She calmed Williams down and asked him to come back the following night to look at the production objectively. When the playwright did so, he agreed that Brando's changes had added new dimensions to both the part and the play.

It was as if new dimensions were being added to Brando's personality, as well, during this period. Depressed and suffering from headaches that would last as long as four days, he felt that he needed professional help. Kazan gave him the name of a psychiatrist, and Brando began a course of analysis that was to last a number of years.

About this time, too, the actor presumably became a motorcycle aficionado. After appearing in *Streetcar* for a year, he was given a handsome bonus; he spent part of it on a huge bike, on which he zoomed around Manhattan and the nearby countryside whenever he had a chance. Quite likely, he drove the bike back to Libertyville, Illinois, during this period to visit his parents. One former Chicago Northsider remembers attending a party at a North Shore mansion at which Brando showed up sporting leather boots and carrying a stunning young woman on the rear of the cycle seat.

Certainly he was having no trouble meeting and squiring New York's most elegant women at this time. For a while, the actor went with a dancer named Tony Parker. In 1948 he announced that he was about to become engaged to Cecelia D'Arthuniaga, a Colombian girl who was a fashion publicist. But matrimony was not the outcome of this or of other brief romances conducted during the time he was a Broadway star. Later, he reasoned that his inability to love stemmed from feelings of inferiority.

Brando undoubtedly had a great many more problems to sort out when he finally left the cast of *Streetcar* in 1949. He was the hottest young actor on Broadway, yet his success seemed unreal to him. Commenting on this period of his life, he later said that he wasn't excited when he "made it," that he'd never thought much about his career in terms of "making it." He had just accepted it as a matter of course. Later, he elaborated further by noting that he had never really realized how big a success he was because he was too involved with his own problems. Then one night when he was doing *Streetcar* in New York, he had heard a roar from the audience, and it was as though he suddenly had awakened to find that he was on top of the heap.

But being on top wasn't enough. Though Brando had arrived, he was seemingly disillusioned. He admitted once, "Working in the theater can be tedious beyond belief. Most people who are behind plays are commercially oriented. The play is product—like toothpaste—they want it standardized, unchanged. But to keep a play alive, an actor cannot stay in the same posture all the time. He must move to other areas to keep his performance from being fatigued and threadbare."

When Brando finally left Broadway, he evidently had no idea of what he really wanted to do. An interviewer asked him about his future plans just before he set sail again for Paris. "I thought I might get a pet raccoon," he told the flabbergasted questioner—adding, when he saw the look on the man's face, "they make wonderful pets, you know."

Offers from Hollywood pursued Brando all the way to Europe. Most of them were uninteresting, but his agent sent him one script that seemed worthwhile. Perhaps the movies would offer him one answer to his professional problems, if not his personal ones. Anyway, there was really only one way to find out, so he finally cabled an affirmative reply to the States.

4.

Enter the Slob

THE CABLES that had been crossing the Atlantic in an effort to tempt Brando to come to Hollywood were from Stanley Kramer, the prestigious producer who had just finished making *The Champion* and *Home of the Brave.* The script that Brando's agent, Jay Kanter, had rushed to him in Paris (where he had reportedly read it one afternoon while stolling from café to café) was written by Carl Foreman. Like that writer's *Home of the Brave,* the new script dealt with the postwar problems of returning veterans—in this case, paraplegics. The movie was to be directed by Fred Zinneman, whose semidocumentary *The Search,* with Montgomery Clift, had attracted wide attention in 1948.

The combination of Kramer, Foreman, and Zinneman probably would have been enough to tempt the most rigid Hollywood holdout. But Brando had received other good offers at this time and had turned them down. He had been considered for the lead in *The Brave Bulls,* for example, but he reportedly had turned the offer down because he didn't approve of bullfighting.

Foreman's script for *The Men* was something different. It had a broad message about the ability of the human spirit to rise above any obstacle, and it attempted to improve society's attitudes toward paraplegics. In addition, it was to be produced in semidocumentary style at the Birmingham Veterans Hospital in Van Nuys, California, using actual paraplegics as members of the cast. Finally, Brando reportedly was to receive $40,000 for his work on a one-picture contract. So what could he lose? It seemed as though he were ready for Hollywood.

Hollywood, however, wasn't quite ready for the twenty-five-year-old nonconformist. When Brando stepped off the train in Los Angeles in August, 1949, to begin work on the picture, he was greeted by his grandmother, aunt, and uncle. At first glance, he seemed like any other young man arriving to undertake a new job. Closer examination, however, revealed to his relatives that Marlon's tweed suit was badly rumpled, with a large tear in one knee, and that he had brought with him only a few T-shirts, a pair of faded jeans, and some battered sneakers. Was this a potential film star?

In California, Brando moved in with his relatives, but one wonders, learning how Brando conducted himself in that small house in Eagle Rock, whether the West Coast branch of the family didn't soon regret their decision to put him up.

First, there was the matter of his dress. Once he removed the suit he had arrived in, it was never seen again. Brando's daily costume was jeans, a T-shirt, and sneakers (usually worn without socks).

Both his family and the studio heads tried to do

something about Brando's clothes. Kramer sometimes gave him money to go out and get a "decent" suit. Brando invariably returned with an outfit he'd selected from the work-clothes rack. Marlon's relatives fared no better than Kramer. One day his aunt and grandmother took him to a Los Angeles department store and bought him a pair of slacks and an expensive wool sweater. He wore the newly purchased outfit as he rode down the store elevator with them, and the women felt they had reformed him. Then, probably to their horror, he struck a match and applied it to the fuzzy surface of the sweater. It blazed up briefly, making him look like a human torch. After that, they gave up trying to change him.

There was also the matter of the young man's eating and sleeping habits. After living a carefree existence with Wally Cox in their pack-rat apartment, Brando had little concern for the niceties of conventional living. He waved off his relatives' suggestions that they fix up a room for him in the house, announcing that he would be perfectly happy sleeping on their couch. All he needed was a blanket and pillow. Of course, they never were sure when or if he was going to use the sofa. His hours were extremely irregular, and his grandmother finally abandoned her practice of waiting up for him.

The old woman told friends at this time, "I just hope Bud comes through this without too much scandal. I'm always afraid that I'll be hearing from him in San Quentin."

When Bud did spend some time at home, there was no mistaking the fact. He'd prepare huge banquets of raw eggs (which he downed by the half-dozen) and gallons of peanut butter. When he was present for a regular family meal, his appetite seemed insatiable. "Why, you'd think the boy was starving," his grandmother observed.

Fortunately for his grandmother's nerves, Brando stayed with them for only a few weeks. After discussing the script with Kramer and Zinneman, Brando, true to his Method experience, asked if he could move into the rehabilitation center and live as a paraplegic until the filming got under way.

Both men were enthusiastic about the idea. They obtained special permission from the hospital authorities and the Paraplegic Veterans' Association (PVA), and the actor moved in. There were some doubts about how Brando would fit in, how the men would react to a Hollywood actor in their midst, but everyone felt it was worth the chance.

Not surprisingly, Brando soon was accepted by the vets. They were enthusiastic about the film that was being planned. Furthermore, they realized that Brando was not just another Hollywood star who had come out to jolly them up with false cheer.

Pat Grissom, then president of PVA at Birmingham, stated, "The guys were tired of the 'cheery' visits of celebrities or the deep-thought approach which viewed them as neurotics. Marlon had a natural approach . . . he saw us as human beings with problems. As a result, the guys have accepted him more as a fellow paraplegic than as an actor."

Brando worked hard at maintaining that image. When he wasn't occupied with physical therapy, he stayed in a hospital bed or a wheelchair. In the exercise room he learned to cover the length of two parallel bars and to climb ropes without the use of his legs. Sometimes he joined the vets in the swimming pool for a game of water polo.

Finally he became so proficient at simulating a paraplegic that he was able to fool even the therapists. When Brando was being fitted for leg braces, for example, a regular at the hospital told an attendant that the actor was paralyzed from the tenth dorsal vertebra down without ever realizing that Brando was actually normal.

The way Brando treated the vets was probably the most important reason for his acceptance. He didn't pity them. Brando, always a lover of jokes, quickly adapted to the hospital's graveyard humor. When one of the paraplegics would tell someone to turn down a blaring radio, for example, another would respond, "Why don't you do it yourself—you paralyzed or something?" (The line later was inserted in the script and used against the character Brando was playing.) When the actor was made the butt of a joke, he gave tit for tat. Once, when he was sleeping peacefully in his adjustable hospital bed, one of the paraplegics rolled up both ends and trapped him in the middle. From his prison Brando reportedly screamed out that he'd drown his tormentor in the pool when he got free.

On one occasion, Brando's success at imitating a paraplegic almost resulted in tragedy. Playing his role to the hilt, he had learned to use a specially equipped car that had only manual controls. He used the vehicle to drive the vets to their favorite watering hole in a nearby town. Halfway to their hangout one night, the car had a flat tire. Brando, the only one in the auto who could fix it, pulled over to the side and prepared to get out. When he tried to stand up, his legs, weakened from weeks of disuse, gave way. He stumbled forward, almost tumbling over a cliff before finally falling flat on his face.

Another night, after arriving at the small nightclub, he and the veterans were sitting quietly, minding their own business, when a woman approached them with biblical tracts. In her zeal she told them that quite possibly they could be cured if they placed their trust in the Lord. Brando, from his wheelchair, asked her if all he needed to be cured was an unquestioning faith.

"That's right, young man. Just put your faith in the Almighty," she exclaimed, her eyes brightening.

Blurting out earnestly that he was a true believer, Brando stripped off his leg braces and raised himself up in the wheelchair. Cautiously, he moved one foot forward, placed his weight on it, then tried his other foot. Letting go his grip on the wheelchair, he inched forward.

"Hallelujah! He's been saved! He can walk!" some of the vets screamed at the astounded woman. Others tried to keep up the front, adding their cries of amazement. It finally became too much for all of them, and they burst into gales of laughter. The woman gave them one terrified look, then bolted out the door.

Brando didn't fool everyone so easily. After the actor's first few weeks of living in a wheelchair, pulling himself in and out of bed without using his legs, one of the vets told Zinneman, who had come out to check on Brando's progress, "He still uses his legs too much when pushing himself out of bed. Also, he sometimes forgets and reaches down to scratch his ankle—you know, paraplegics have no feeling below the waist."

Brando kept at it for more than a month. The effort was a great deal harder than he had thought it would be. "Everywhere you think of going," he said, "you have to plot your course in advance and figure—are there steps there? What about doorways? Are there elevators?"

Finally, however, the vets who had been tutoring Brando felt he was ready. He had mastered the actions of a paraplegic and also had found his character: Ken, the bitter returning vet. However, there was something about Brando's delivery that didn't suit a Ken *Williams*— probably a carryover from two years of playing Kowalski—so the studio decided to change the character's last name to Wilozek.

Only one part of the movie really bothered Brando: the scene in which Ken's college sweetheart comes to the hospital, against his wishes, to visit him for the first time. Would he "feel" the scene too much? Would the scene look overplayed on the screen? Luther Adler once had told Brando: "Hold back twenty percent of what is going on inside you and you'll always be honest with an audience. They're the actors, after all. Try to show them more than that and they'll feel you're not being square with them." It proved to be good advice.

When the time came to shoot the scene, Zinneman and Kramer held their breaths. Brando and Teresa Wright, who played Ken's sweetheart, had run through the scene a few times, and each time there had been a subtle difference. The producer and director didn't know what to expect on the first take. The cameras began to roll as Wright entered the darkened hospital ward. Brando lay quietly, apparently lost in thought, not acknowledging her presence until she was near the bed. Seeing her, he turned his head away, as if trying to escape; then, as she spoke to him, he lashed out at her, screaming at her to go away. Finally, the two became reconciled. The camera did a slow fade, and a general cheer went up. Everyone was deeply touched by Brando's performance. Teresa Wright was moved to tears.

The reaction of the critics when the film appeared in the spring of 1950 was enthusiastic. Manny Farber in the *Nation* correctly predicted that Brando's "throwaway tactics may swerve naturalistic acting from deadpan to florid and produce a new tribe of instinctual fire-balls." John Mason Brown in the *Saturday Review* placed the film in the same category as *The Lost Week-*

end, The Snake Pit, and *All the King's Men* because of its willingness to deal with grim reality. Brown called Brando "outstanding and unforgettable," adding that his face was a "seismograph of volcanic emotions." Calling the picture a "fine and arresting film drama," Bosley Crowther in the *New York Times* had this to say about Brando's performance: "[He] is so vividly real, dynamic, and sensitive that his illusion is complete." As for Brando's diction, the critic noted that the actor was "articulate in every way."

Some observers, quite justly, criticized the preachy, simplistic quality of the film. Basically the story of how a man faced with a lifetime in a wheelchair and dependency on others finally makes peace with himself and accepts his fate, it sometimes makes its points too obviously. But it was billed as a "semidocumentary," and, as such, perhaps some heavy-handedness may be excused.

In any case, most observers were unanimous in their praise for both the film and the new star. Just how enthusiastic they were can be seen from the fact that Brando received an Academy Award nomination for his role. (Ultimately, he lost out to Jose Ferrer, who played the poet with the proboscis in *Cyrano de Bergerac.*)

Despite the fact that the critics and public had taken to the new star, Brando was still bad news to the Hollywood establishment. At first, columnists who had trouble getting to him dubbed him the Male Garbo. Later, after some of them had done their homework and discovered what a sensation he had been in *Streetcar* as a new kind of sex symbol, they changed Brando's title to the New Valentino. Finally—after he had given several interviews in his usual grubby attire, called Hollywood a "cultural graveyard," said the studio starlets were "sticky," and sometimes yawned or scratched himself as the reporters sat with their pencils poised—they seemed to agree on one final term: the Slob.

It is easy to see why Brando upset columnists. For the first time, they were faced with a star who simply wouldn't play the game. He tore around the Los Angeles countryside on a motorcycle. He stayed away from the usual studio crowd, dating waitresses and secretaries. Sometimes—horrors!—he didn't even bother to wear shoes. And to make matters worse, he constantly was putting the writers on. He told one interviewer that his parents were destitute Polish displaced persons who were living on relief. Another looked at him wide-eyed when he informed her that he ate mainly gazelles' eyes.

Perhaps his worst offense was the way he treated the two most important columnists of the day, Hedda Hopper and Louella Parsons. It was bad enough that he never mentioned them by name, referring to them always as "the One with the Hats" and "the Fat One." More unforgivable was the way he treated them when he finally granted an interview. At his first meeting with Hopper—on the set of *The Men*—he reportedly answered her endless questions with nothing but grunts. In her column, she graciously attributed his responses to his absorption in the role he was playing. When Parsons first saw Brando and gushed that he looked just like any other average American boy, the story goes that he went off in a corner of the studio and stood on his head.

The few reporters who were able to talk with Brando at the studio felt that they were lucky—even if they came away with only a couple of grunts and some unquotable material. Most writers found that the typical Brando interview was given in some remote part of the Los Angeles countryside—and then only after the star had walked the writer over some rough terrain.

Brando's opinions were outrageous for an up-and-coming star. For example, when asked to name his favorite films and actors, he mentioned De Sica's *The Bicycle Thief*, Gerrard Philipe, and Jean-Louis Barrault. Good God, these weren't even Hollywood products! When he did get around to discussing the American movie capitol, the reporters wished he hadn't. He told one writer, "All I see out here are a bunch of funnies riding around in satin Cadillacs." To another he admitted, "The only reason I'm here is because I don't have the moral strength to turn down the money."

What about the noble profession of acting? he was asked continually. He replied, "I have no respect for acting. By and large, it's the expression of a neurotic impulse. It's a bum's life—you get paid for doing nothing, and it means nothing. My advice to a young actor is to give it up—that is a sign of maturity. Because it's really a childish thing to do."

But certainly acting takes skill and sensitivity, the columnists kept insisting. Again, Brando undercut them, saying that most people are born actors because almost everybody lies, and acting is lying.

When the writers asked how acting on the stage differed from working in movies, Brando explained, "I'll show you Hollywood. Say you're watching someone die. Here's the camera. Meanwhile you're supposed to register some emotion by looking off at something—like a half-eaten orange. Maybe just a pencil. Hollywood isn't conducive to relaxed production. It's all wrapped up in precision, mechanics, and they're always racing for time. On the stage you at least can take a running jump at a role."

To make the reporters even more uncomfortable, Brando often would tell them that he only meant half of what he said.

In a way, Brando threatened the whole concept of the star system. Stars were supposed to be made by studios, by tireless press agents, by the power the gossip columnists and movie commentators wielded over the fans. But along had come a young actor with real talent who made fun of the whole setup. And the movie-going public was still interested in him. Suppose the other stars caught on?

When it came right down to it, the studio heads realized that they didn't have much choice—at least not while Brando was so hot at the box office. At least that's the way Jack Warner figured it when he obtained the film rights to *Streetcar*. In early spring, 1950, when the outspoken studio boss had a conference with Elia Kazan (who was to direct the movie version of the Broadway hit), both knew that they simply *had* to have Brando for the role of Kowalski. Warner was worried about keeping the young star under control, but the director told him that he could keep Brando in line by being firm with him. And he pointed out that the technicians on the set of *The Men* said that they'd never seen any newcomer pick up on the fine points of working before a camera as quickly as Brando.

There was also the question of money. In the past, Warner had signed promising new stars to long-term contracts. But those days were over. When negotiations for *Streetcar* ended, Warner was forced to come up with a whopping $75,000 for Brando on a one-picture basis.

Considering the amount of money that Brando was earning at this time, he should have been living like a prince. But he wasn't. He managed on the $150 allowance that his father, who had taken over the management of his business affairs, doled out to him every week. Brando didn't have any fancy clothes, big cars, or expensive hobbies. When he took a girl out, it was usually for an afternoon at the zoo or a night at the movies, with a hamburger and shake afterward.

With so little to spend, Brando spent his money almost as fast as it came in. And so he was always broke. It didn't help matters that the standard joke around the studio was that lending money to Brando was like pouring it down a sewer, and everyone wised up pretty quickly.

His father, fortunately, was an expert money manager. One of the first of the many investments that he made for his son was the Pennypoke Farm, forty acres of rolling countryside just outside Mundelein, Illinois. Frannie Brando and her husband were to settle there in 1953.

Back in 1950, Brando didn't seem too concerned with investments and future holdings. He did enjoy the Midwest, and he went home to see his family whenever he could. Just before *The Men* came out, he was seen around Libertyville getting in touch with old friends and buying supplies to help fix up his parents' new home. The local newspaper, the *Libertyville Independent Register,* sent a reporter to interview the new celebrity.

As usual, Brando couldn't resist putting the writer on. After describing the roles he'd played on Broadway and his work in *The Men,* Brando added that he'd also won the Pulitzer Prize for writing something called "The Critics of War." Or at least, that's how the reporter wrote up the information.

It was also around this time—just before Brando began work on the film version of *Streetcar*—that the actor acquired Russell, a pet raccoon. Brando still maintained an apartment with Cox in New York. But when Russell cut his permanent teeth on Wally's only suit, Cox moved out in a huff. Brando consoled himself by taking long walks around Manhattan with his new roommate perched on his shoulder.

Filming *Streetcar* was scheduled to begin in August, 1950. Recreating the roles they had perfected on Broadway were Kim Hunter and Karl Malden. With Brando playing the male lead, it was like old-home week.

The studio heads were a bit concerned as to whether Vivien Leigh, cast as Blanche, would be able to work with the tight-knit group. Vivien Leigh hadn't appeared in a Hollywood film since 1941, and Blanche was a far distance from her last role as Nelson's Lady Hamilton.

As things turned out, no one need have worried. Karl Malden later commented: "At first I thought it would be difficult working ourselves in. I'm the kind of guy who likes to be completely relaxed with the other players. The gang from the play were all friends from New York and Vivien was the only outsider. We got together beforehand and decided to go all out to make her feel at home. We needn't have bothered. As soon as she walked on the set, we all got along beautifully."

Some of the Hollywood commentators billed the Leigh-Brando combination as the "meeting of the lady and the tiger." Vivien Leigh, when questioned about working with Brando, said sweetly, "Mr. Brando is only a tiger when the role demands it."

Although the cast got along beautifully, the studio heads were having other problems. They were worried that Williams's screenplay would not meet the standards of the Movie Production Code. If *Streetcar* did not receive an approved rating or if the Catholic church condemned the film, the box office could be in serious trouble.

For the film version of *Streetcar,* the rape scene

between Stanley and Blanche was eliminated, the homosexuality of Blanche's dead husband was glossed over, the language was bowdlerized, and the sexual relationship between Stella and Stanley was played down. Even the ending was changed so that Stanley finally lost Stella. These revisions toned down the script considerably, but *Streetcar* was still pretty rough stuff for its day.

Nevertheless, the production went ahead full steam. A replica of the Broadway set was erected on the Warner Brothers lot. Kazan set to work, figuring his camera angles, coaching his cast, and trying his best to capture the flavor of the Broadway show.

Using tight shots and closeups, the director focused mainly on his principals. With the exception of the opening scene and the scene in which Blanche and Mitch go out for a night on the town, the action was confined to the set to achieve the dramatic intensity of the play.

When the movie was finished, Kazan was satisfied that he'd done his best considering the limitations under which he was working. The film was scheduled to open at the Radio City Music Hall in the summer of 1951. Then, surprisingly, the opening night was canceled.

Behind the scenes, things were happening. Warner Brothers had received advance notice that the Catholic church's Legion of Decency was going to give the film a condemned rating. The studio feared picketing, boycotts, and trouble with local censors (still powerful in those days).

Unknown to Kazan, the studio then hired a Catholic layperson to edit the film and remove any "offending" material. The music supporting the big love scene between Stella and Stanley was cut because the editor felt it made their relationship too carnal. The line preceding Stanley's attack upon Blanche—"You know, you might not be bad to interfere with"—was dropped.

And certain of Stella's critical reactions were cut to make her seem more like a "good girl."

There were twelve cuts in all, amounting only to some four minutes. But when Kazan saw the edited version, he stated that the heart had been cut out of a work of art. The transformation of Stella into a goody-goody, for example, made no sense and was in conflict with the main action of the play. As for the other cuts, they simply destroyed both the continuity and the mood the director had worked so hard to establish.

Despite the studio's last-minute editing, the critics were unanimous in their praise of the film. Better yet from the studio's viewpoint, *Streetcar* broke all box-office records.

Bosley Crowther called the film a "motion picture that throbs with passion and poignancy," adding that it compared favorably with the play. The critic applauded the superlative performance of Vivien Leigh and continued:

No less brilliant, however, within his area, is Marlon Brando in the role of the loud, lusty, brawling, brutal, amoral Polish brother-in-law. Mr. Brando created the role in the stage play, and he carries over all the energy and the steel-spring characteristics that make him vivid on the stage. But here, where we're so much closer to him, he seems that much more highly charged, his despairs seem that much more pathetic, and his comic movements that much more slyly enjoyed.

Life's reviewer said that the star "fills the screen with immense energy," while Robert Hatch reflected in the *Nation:* "Brando's Kowalski is not so much a throwback as a Neanderthal genius thrust eons into the future." Hollis Alpert in the *Saturday Review* maintained that Brando's performance had "overwhelming impact."

When it came time for the Oscar presentations the following spring, Brando was again in the running for Best Actor. Also vying for the award were Montgomery Clift and Humphrey Bogart. Most felt that the younger men were more deserving. Clift had earned substantial critical acclaim for his portrait of the tragic loser in *A Place in the Sun,* while Bogart had more or less walked through his role of the disreputable tugboat captain in *The African Queen.* On the other hand, the smart money was on Bogey since the Academy had slighted him when it had overlooked his monumental performance in *Treasure of Sierra Madre.*

When the votes were tallied, sentiment won out, and Bogey received his first Oscar. George Stevens was named Best Director for *A Place in the Sun,* and Karl Malden and Kim Hunter from *Streetcar* picked up Oscars for Best Supporting Actor and Best Supporting Actress. The film that walked off with top honors was the musical *An American in Paris.*

Analyzing this surprising turn of events, Crowther explained that while the Hollywood highbrows were splitting their votes between the pictures of Kazan and Stevens, the middle-brow contingent lined up solidly behind the pseudo-biography of George Gershwin. Metro, the studio that produced *An American in Paris,* was so taken aback by its luck that it ran an ad in *Variety* showing Leo the Lion with an Oscar in his paws under the caption, "Honestly, I was just standing in The Sun waiting for a Streetcar."

By the time Hunter and Malden picked up their Oscars for *Streetcar,* Brando had already finished his third picture, one that was to earn him his third consecutive Academy Award nomination. Shooting of *Viva Zapata!* had begun in spring, 1951. But the history of the film goes back quite some time prior to that.

The idea for a movie biography of the revolutionary Mexican leader and folk hero originated in a phone call between John Steinbeck, the novelist, and Kazan sometime in 1949. At the time, Steinbeck was interested in the diaries of Christopher Columbus, and he suggested that a film be made about the Italian explorer. Kazan informed him that another studio was already doing such a film, starring Fredric March. The conversation drifted to the Mexican revolution and a biography of Emiliano Zapata that had just been published. The character of Zapata intrigued Steinbeck, and he proposed to investigate the subject further. Within a few months he came up with a script that Kazan felt would make a fine film.

According to Kazan, he and Steinbeck were particularly interested in the fact that although Zapata was a revolutionary, he was too much of an idealist to be effective. When Zapata discovered that to implement his programs he would have to become as cruel as the regime he had overthrown, he turned his back on power and returned to his people.

Critics and historians were quick to attack this basic assumption. The more radical press saw in the film (and especially in the mysterious character of Fernando, as played by Joseph Wiseman, a kind of archetypal Communist) a thinly veiled attack on communism. Historians pointed out that Zapata had been driven from Mexico City after gaining power by forces other than his own idealism. Some observers saw the film as an effort on the part of Kazan and Steinbeck to redeem themselves in the eyes of the repressive House Un-American Activities Committee from their former associations with radical groups and causes.

Whether or not the thesis and facts of the film were

historically valid, Brando threw himself into the role with great enthusiasm. He had signed a new contract with Twentieth Century-Fox (which was to cause him some trouble later, as we shall see) and was to earn $100,000 for his portrayal of Zapata.

As part of his homework, Brando read everything he could find about the Mexican revolutionary, including the biography on which Steinbeck based his script, *Zapata the Unconquerable,* by Edgcumb Pinchon. Brando also began working on a Mexican accent, which he used both on and off the set. Finally, he brought in Phil Rhodes, his own makeup man, from New York to make himself look the part of a Mexican peasant with Indian blood.

Brando worked hard to create the role of Zapata, but, characteristically, he also played hard. For one thing, he brought his raccoon with him when filming started on the Texas side of the Rio Grande. Russell had already come between Brando and Cox, and the raccoon was almost the cause of a rift between his owner and another friend. When Jean Peters, Brando's leading lady, offered to take the actor for a spin in her new convertible, Brando took his pet along and Russell left a sizable puddle on the rear seat of the car. The actress was furious when she discovered it, but Brando calmed her down by pointing out that the raccoon was only a baby.

Miss Peters relented, and the friendship continued. In fact, Brando appeared to be somewhat enamored of her during the first few weeks of shooting. One night, guitar in hand, he climbed a tree under her hotel window and began serenading her—at three in the morning! But the romance never really developed, and after the film was completed, the young actress said only, "He's one of the greatest people I've ever worked with—everyone loved him, the cast and the crew."

The wee-hours balladeering, among other things, made people wonder about Brando. They were, by now, prepared to overlook the fact that he arrived on location with only a couple of T-shirts, that he borrowed clothing from anyone his size, that his raccoon was mischievous and smelly, and that he practiced yoga on the front lawn of his hotel. But could they cope with the firecrackers that Brando set off in the hotel lobby? His water fights with the crew? And then there was the time he gave Kazan a real scare; after he had been gunned down at the end of the film, he just lay there on the dusty ground. Had the tech crew forgotten to put blanks in the guns? Brando jumped up, grinning, when the director rushed over to see if he were still alive.

Brando's antics only confirmed the fears that many of the studio heads had expressed when Kazan informed them that he had to have Brando for the part of Zapata. The executives had argued, but Kazan had insisted that he wouldn't do the picture without Brando. When the director screened the first rushes of the film, he gushed, "Look at that face—that face! The brooding sadness of it, the poetry. Jesus, it's the face of an Edgar Allen Poe!" The studio heads had to agree.

When the film was released, the critics also backed up Kazan's opinion of his star. In *Saturday Review* Hollis Alpert was negative on the picture but found Brando, with his flared nostrils (achieved with plastic bands in his nose) and glued-down eyelid corners, "convincing and powerful." Laura Hobson in her column in the same magazine found the picture "sensitive, stirring, and noble." In the *New York Times* Crowther praised the picture generally and said that Brando's portrayal had "power enough to cause the screen to throb."

Later, Crowther named the film as one of the best of 1952. When the votes of the Academy were tallied, however, Brando lost out again for Best Actor—this time to another old sentimental favorite, Gary Cooper, for his performance in *High Noon.*

Actually, Brando seemed totally uninterested in Hollywood's graven little image. After finishing *Zapata,* he returned to New York, where he did a television show in which he played the role of a prizefighter. Characteristically, to get the feel of the part, he worked out every day at Stillman's Gym with a middleweight pro.

In fact, Brando's friends in New York found him, at least superficially, the same as he had always been. John Lardner, who wrote the script for the television show Brando did, commented that the first time he saw the new Hollywood star, Brando was sliding down a bannister in the New York subway.

Indeed, despite the fact that Russell was still with him, Brando patched up his friendship with Cox, telling Wally about an exotic Mexican actress, an extra in *Zapata,* who was coming from Mexico to see him.

Brando evidently said no more about this until she arrived. Then he introduced her only as Movita. She was still quite a beauty, though a few years older than Brando. How much older has never been revealed, but it is significant that the Mexican star, who was to figure importantly later in Brando's life, had played the role of Franchot Tone's Tahitian sweetheart in the filming of *Mutiny on the Bounty* in 1935! At that time, her name had been Maria Castaneda.

Though Brando appeared to be serious about Movita, he was apparently not ready to make a lasting commitment. Instead, he announced that he was going to do a bit of traveling and think things over. As usual, this meant a trip back to Paris and Europe. In New York he couldn't get away from his agent and the motion picture and television executives who continually bombarded him with offers.

All of the proposals he received apparently were uninteresting. He seemed to be trying desperately to remain the same person he had been before his success with *Streetcar*. But in 1952, after extensive analysis and with the demands that his successes had foisted upon him, that seemed less and less possible.

5.

Et Tu, Oscar

BY THE middle of 1952, Brando was prob-
ably more uncertain than ever about whether he wanted
to continue acting, and he also seemed to be growing
suspicious that Hollywood was using him. True, his first
three pictures had provided him with choice parts. But,
as some critics had asked, was there really that much difference between Ken Wilozek, Stanley Kowalski, and
Amiliano Zapata?

When it came right down to it, all three characters
were of a type: brooding, impulsive, inarticulate, explosive. It is, therefore, not unreasonable to assume that,
despite the fact that Brando's work had been good
enough to win him three consecutive Academy Award
nominations, in the back of his mind was the fear that
he was already being typecast.

Then, toward the end of the summer of 1952, Brando's agent began getting feelers from director Joseph

Mankiewicz and producer John Houseman about something really different. It was an extremely prestigious role, one that would demand a great deal of work on Brando's part and one that had certain drawbacks.

Brando was reportedly amazed when he was asked to play Mark Antony in the movie version of Shakespeare's *Julius Caesar*. But his agent advised him that it was really the case. Evidently, John Houseman, the producer, had seen Brando's performance in *A Flag Is Born* and had been impressed by his diction and delivery.

There was a catch in the offer, however, since this was to be a low-budget picture — albeit a prestigious one. Other stars such as John Gielgud, James Mason, and Louis Calhern had agreed to work for far less than their customary fees in order to get the picture out. It didn't matter. Brando quickly accepted the invitation to join the all-star cast.

The press had a field day when they heard the news. So the Mumbler was going to try his hand at Shakespeare. It was going to be fun to see the cocky kid take a well-deserved pratfall.

Unfortunately for such snipers, Mankiewicz maintained a rigidly closed set once filming started. When the press caught up with the director after hours and began making sly digs about Brando, he told them through a cloud of cigar smoke, "Don't get caught with the scoffers; you might be very embarrassed."

When the press found Brando and asked him about the role, he admitted freely that he had the jitters — but no more so than with any other picture that was getting under way.

The studio heads at MGM were holding their breaths. Shakespeare didn't have a good track record at the box office. In 1935 Warner Brothers had just managed to scrape by with the Max Reinhardt production of *A Midsummer Night's Dream,* starring James Cagney. But MGM had lost a quarter-million dollars on their attempt at *Romeo and Juliet,* featuring Norma Shearer and Leslie Howard. On the plus side, of course, there were always Olivier's *Henry V* and *Hamlet* (1944 and 1948, respectively). However, Olivier was something special, and both films had been done in Technicolor.

Mankiewicz insisted that the film be shot in black and white not only to keep within his slim $2-million budget, but for artistic reasons. He wanted starkness, an atmosphere of shadows and contrasting textures, to heighten the mood of the film.

As for Brando, he worked overtime to prepare for the role. Using a tape recorder, he worked along with Mankiewicz to perfect the modified British accent the director wanted. In addition, he drilled with Gertrude Folger, MGM's speech coach from Boston, for six long, grueling weeks.

When asked about her pupil, his coach commented, "The jibes about his diction are unjust. If he's playing a slovenly character, his diction quite properly fits. But his own is excellent."

The tiny, bird-like coach also compared working with the supposed bad-boy to some of the other stars whom she had helped in the past: "Such a dear boy, so punctual, so modest, so willing. I can't remember when I've had such a hard-working, keen, rewarding pupil. He's always prepared and considerate, and, unlike some big stars—who sometimes just don't show up—he always phones if he's going to be late."

Mankiewicz, too, was impressed by Brando's work habits. The young actor listened closely and took direction well; he also was usually the first one on the set.

Gielgud was probably a bit miffed at this since he had built a reputation for always being the first to arrive in the morning.

Friendly rivalry was in keeping with the generally happy and optimistic atmosphere on the lot. Brando refrained from his usual antics—perhaps out of consideration for the more staid and prestigious members of the cast. He, himself, took quite a bit of ribbing over the fact that his hair was thinning appreciably in front.

Calhern told Brando one day that there was only one thing that bothered him about his portrayal of Mark Antony. When the alarmed Brando asked Calhern what the problem was, the film's Caesar replied that Antony was bald as a billiard ball. "But maybe there's some hope yet," Calhern teased.

Others in the cast had more serious worries. Gielgud, for example, was concerned about what the writers would do with his beloved Shakespeare. In addition, he seemed anxious about his own performance. He had played the role of Cassius two years previously in England at Stratford-on-Avon. But that had been on stage. This time he was in front of a camera, and it had been twelve years since he had appeared in a movie. Furthermore, there was a notable disparity between his accent and Brando's.

When Gielgud was asked later how Mankiewicz had solved this last problem and whether he was satisfied with the end result, the actor replied, "Mankiewicz was somehow able to tone my accent down while heightening Brando's. As far as the overall product is concerned, I was struck by how the script of the play was respected and adapted to the screen. Shakespeare would certainly be delighted."

The opening night audience in Sydney, Australia, agreed with the Shakespearean star. The world premier, which was a "first" for a Hollywood film in the land down-under, was a huge financial and critical success. Though it had been ready for distribution the previous winter, the film did not premier until May, 1953. Doubtless, MGM held back to obtain maximum coverage during the slow summer season, and, of course, there was the additional ploy of building up suspense.

At any rate, when *Julius Caesar* finally opened in New York in June, 1953, it created quite a sensation. A photograph of Brando in a Roman toga appeared on the cover of *Life,* and the magazine featured a number of magnificent production shots of the film in a lengthy spread.

For the most part, the critics praised the picture highly. Crowther called it a "stirring and memorable film," adding, ". . . The delight and surprise of the film is Mr. Brando's Mark Antony, which is something memorable to see. Athletic and bullet-headed, he looks the realest Roman of them all and possesses the fire of hot convictions and the firm elasticity of steel. Happily, Mr. Brando's diction, which has been guttural and slurred in previous films, is clear and precise in this instance. In him, a major talent has emerged."

Other critics followed suit. Alpert wrote in the *Saturday Review* that the film was better than Olivier's *Hamlet.* He found Brando's portrayal "magnificent" and the famous oration scene "stunning."

Eric Bentley in the *New Republic* concurred, calling the picture the "best Shakespearian film to date." Of Brando he wrote, "One always listens to him because his special temperament and keenness are in the lines." In the same review, however, he maintained that the actor could not handle blank verse.

Other critics followed Bentley's lead. Parker Tyler in *Theater Arts* compared the production unfavorably with the 1937 Orson Welles Mercury Theater offering and indicated that Brando's diction left a great deal to be desired: "At times he sounds as if a wad of gum lurked in his jaws."

Despite such evaluations on the part of American critics, Brando's performance and the picture in general were highly praised in England, where Bardophiles are more common—and demanding. In Mexico the film won the Silver Eagle (the equivalent of the Oscar) from the Mexican Motion Picture Critics' Association.

The American Shakespeare Festival honored Mankiewicz and Houseman for their efforts on the production, and Brando was again nominated for the Academy Award, though he lost out this time to William Holden for his portrayal of the cigar-chewing American prisoner of war in *Stalag 17.*

Subtle changes were taking place in Brando at this time. He still seemed undecided about devoting his life to acting, but he also apparently realized that the enormous amounts of money the profession offered could provide him with the lifestyle he wanted. When asked if there wasn't something hypocritical about disparaging his profession and railing against American materialism while at the same time reaping their benefits, Brando answered, "I don't think making money is sinful. When it gets you, rather than you getting it, that's immoral. It makes me sick to think that if you're poor in America, you're some kind of criminal."

About Hollywood his position was that the movie capital was made up largely of talented "money-grubbers." He also noted that it contained a great many actors with great ambitions, refined sensibilities, and no acting talent. On the whole, he stated, most of the people in Hollywood were failures as human beings. His goal, he maintained, was to achieve just a pinch of success without getting sucked into the movie-idol maelstrom, which could be disastrous to an actor.

For the present, then, he told one columnist he wanted to do a few more pictures, achieve some kind of independence, and then travel some and settle down. He wanted a simple life but admitted that such an existence is harder and harder to secure every day.

But the idyllic, carefree existence that Marlon occasionally dreamed about was out of the question for the time being. Mankiewicz was singing the actor's praises everywhere. He told one movie commentator, "When Brando goes into a role, he plunges in like a deep-sea diver. If he was going to play a blind man, he'd go around for weeks with his eyes shut. If he was going to play a man with his right arm missing, he'd do everything lefty until he got the hang of how it felt."

The offers poured in, not only from producers and directors, but from actors who had worked with him. Rumor had it, for example, that John Gielgud wanted Brando to come to England to star in a production of *Hamlet.*

But Brando had other commitments. One of these was to Twentieth Century-Fox under the terms of the contract he had signed when he did *Zapata.* The studio wanted him to lead a cast of thousands in an epic based on a best-selling historical potboiler titled *The Egyptian.* The more Brando thought about it, the more he disliked the idea.

Meanwhile, Stanley Kramer, who had worked with Brando on *The Men,* was after him again. The producer had a script based on a short story titled "Cyclist's Raid," which recounted the actual invasion of a small, sleepy town in southern California by a motorcycle gang. Kramer felt that the film could make some important statements about the rebellious youth subculture that was just becoming visible. And who would be more natural for the part of the motorcycle-gang leader than Brando? After all, didn't he belong to the subculture himself? Wasn't he a rebel who spent a lot of his time tearing around on a chopper?

Brando's acceptance of the role of the leather-jacketed and booted Johnny in *The Wild One* was to have a contradictory effect on his career. On the one hand, it made him an even bigger box-office attraction. One distributor said at the time, "I don't care if the guy is a slob or a Valentino, he's got something, and it's bringing the kids back into the houses." In addition, the film was to become a kind of bench mark picture, one that established a genre. It was the first to open the eyes of the public to the kind of seething rebelliousness that had just begun to boil up between the cracks of a society that was slowly beginning to crumble.

On the other hand, since the role of Johnny was so close to those of Wilozek, Kowalski, and Zapata, the effect of his outstanding performance in *Julius Caesar* was almost vitiated. After *The Wild One,* Brando became largely stereotyped as an inarticulate brute who lashes out without care for the consequences of his actions.

The film opens on an empty road; Brando's voice is heard as the credits unwind: "Once the trouble was on the way," he intones, "I just went along with it." Ironically, the words in some ways parallel Brando's own relationship to the picture. As filming progressed, he realized that the picture was straying from its original purpose. Later he commented, "We started out trying to say something about the hipster psychology, but somewhere along the line we ran off the track. So, in the end, instead of showing why young people tend to join groups that seek expression in violence, we merely showed the violence."

Looking back, it is easy to see the film's flaws. Though the performances of Brando and Lee Marvin (playing a rival gang leader) are first-rate and memorable, the characters of the townspeople and the "good girl" who tries to "save" Johnny are flat and stereotypical.

Nevertheless, some critics were able to look beyond the stock bad-boy-good-girl plot to evaluate the underlying message of the picture. Alpert in the *Saturday Review* praised the film's "startling freshness," calling Brando's performance "astonishing." "Lying behind his bravado," Alpert wrote, "you see the crazy, hurt, messed-up child."

Commentary found the work "powerful and frightening," though the reviewer was critical of the picture's inconclusiveness. As for Brando, the review read, "He turns in another rough, unpleasant characterization, which at times is brilliant."

Crowther, putting his finger deftly on the weaknesses of the film, still found *The Wild One* "tough and engrossing, weird and cruel, while it stays on the beam." Delving into Johnny's psyche, Crowther wrote, " . . . In this taut and eerie hoodlum is fleetingly but forcibly revealed the consequences of youthful frustrations recompensed by association with a cult. Mr. Brando is vicious and relentless so long as he is permitted to be: he barely exposes his battered ego from behind a ferocious front."

The praise seemingly meant little to the introspective star. Ironically, though the role became one of his most famous and the one that engendered the greatest adulation among his younger fans (not to mention the impact it would have on another generation's revolutionary tendencies—posters of him in his leather jacket and motorcycle cap are still selling well in today's "head" shops), it became the film of which Brando was least proud in later years. And for the first time he didn't receive an Oscar nomination for his year's work. Immediately after making *The Wild One,* perhaps to get the taste of the role out of his mouth, Brando did attempt to do something that he considered more artistically challenging and worthwhile. Many people think that Brando's stage career ended with his long stint on Broadway in *Streetcar.* But in 1953 he went back on the boards in a summer theater in Farmingham, Massachusetts.

The play Brando chose for his theater comeback was Shaw's *Arms and the Man.* As the big name in the production, he probably had his choice of the two leading men's roles. Surprisingly, he decided to play Sergius, the aristocratic Bulgarian major with Byronic pretensions, instead of the more pragmatic, antiromantic Bluntschli.

The role of Sergius, like that of Marchbanks in *Candida,* gave Brando a great deal of pleasure. Besides, it was the exact opposite of his film stereotype, and it offered him a chance to test his acting ability.

No noteworthy critical evaluations of Brando's portrayal survive. But William Redfield, who played Bluntschli, states in his *Letter from an Actor* that Brando's work over the run of the play was uneven. One week he would be brilliant, according to Redfield, while the next he would seem nervous and disturbed. When Redfield allegedly chided Brando, stating that some audiences felt that he was laughing at them, Brando reportedly said, "Man, don't you get it? This is summer stock."

The quote was later refuted (as was Redfield's appraisal of Brando's work on the Farmingham stage) by others connected with the production.

Hollywood wasn't too interested in Brando's brief reappearance on the stage or his desire to enlarge his repertory of characters. The Slob as a high-flown fop? The man must be even crazier than he seemed.

As 1953 drew to a close, Brando was offered a role that had all sorts of advantages. It was clearly perfect for him, and it seemed very likely that the role would win him an Oscar. Furthermore, Kazan was directing. It was he who offered Brando the part.

The project was attractive for other reasons. Budd Schulberg had written the script. Leonard Bernstein had agreed to do the background music—his first attempt at scoring a film. Karl Malden would play a supporting role as would Rod Steiger, another Method actor. Finally, the work would be an exposé of criminal activity on the New York waterfront; the script had an important message and serious social implications.

Perhaps it was this last quality of the script that convinced Brando to take the part of Terry Malloy in *On the Waterfront*. The actor had often championed the underdog as a youth, and it appeared to become increasingly important to him as an adult to use his art for socially beneficial purposes.

The history of *Waterfront* was long and stormy. The idea for the film had grown out of a Pulitzer Prize-winning series by New York reporter Malcolm Johnson on the corruption in the New York dockworkers' union. The series showed how criminals and union bosses had joined forces to keep the workers in a state of perpetual terror and serfdom.

Budd Schulberg had been approached by Kazan to do a script based on Johnson's series as far back as 1951.

Schulberg did his homework well, not only obtaining all published information on the subject, but haunting waterfront bars and other hangouts where dockworkers gathered. He talked to priests in the area, union officials, and many others whose lives had been touched by the corruption.

Later that same year, Schulberg presented the finished script to Kazan. Time went by without any action. The director was unable to get any backers; many felt that the story was too controversial. Others maintained that it would be impossible to make the film on location since the gangs and their supporters who ruled the waterfront would never allow a cast and crew to get within shooting distance. And even if they could film on location, a protesting dockworkers' union could cause costly labor troubles. A few potential backers, though uncertain, asked for a rewrite.

Schulberg revamped the script eight times and still it was turned down again and again by the major studios. Kazan finally showed it to Sam Spiegel, an independent producer who had just scored with *The African Queen*. Spiegel liked the Schulberg script immediately and said that he wanted to do it. But he took the precaution of changing his name unofficially to S. P. Eagle for the production.

At this point, Kazan had not fixed on Brando for the lead. For one thing, the star was having contract troubles with Twentieth Century-Fox. For another, Spiegel felt that Frank Sinatra, fresh from his success with the role of Maggio in *From Here to Eternity*, was the man for the part.

Sinatra wanted the role. And when he found out that the role had been given to Brando, he stopped speaking to Spiegel. Eventually, he went even further, suing

Spiegel—unsuccessfully—for $500,000 for backing out of the deal.

Despite his Twentieth Century-Fox contractual difficulties, Brando agreed to take the part. He immediately began to work on a Bronx accent and spent his off-hours at waterfront dives or standing around watching dockworkers unloading ships. His success in fleshing out the character of Terry almost got him into serious trouble when he stopped in at a dingy joint to do some people-watching one night on his way home. As he was sitting there, the police stormed in on a narcotics raid. Brando tried to tell them who he was, but they looked at him in disbelief and made him roll up his sleeves so that they could look for the telltale puncture marks of an addict.

Kazan and Spiegel received a number of anonymous threats before actual shooting began on the docks of Hoboken, New Jersey. It was hinted that there would be labor troubles once the picture got under way, that mobsters would never allow Kazan to move his equipment and cast to the waterfront location, that those connected with the venture would suffer reprisals from the Mob.

Courageously, the film's producer and director went ahead. Even the fact that a number of apparent mobsters actually showed up on the waterfront location didn't deter them. Kazan and Spiegel hired their own corps of bodyguards to see that the silent critics didn't get out of hand. In fact, Kazan got so used to the mobsters' presence that occasionally, after finishing a scene, he would ask them if any detail had been overlooked. They offered no help; the most they would do was grunt a noncommittal reply.

Kazan went even further than shooting on location to

instill the film with realism. He hired former boxers Tony ("Two Ton") Galento, Abe Simon, and Tami Mauriello to play union goons. He also employed Anthony ("Tony Mike") De Vincenzo, a waterfront hiring boss who had testified before a state crime committee in connection with the dock scandal, as a consultant. (After *Waterfront* was released, De Vincenzo unsuccessfully attempted to sue Spiegel for invasion of privacy, alleging that the plot and principal character of the film had been based on his life.)

The weeks of shooting rolled on without any trouble from expected sources. Whatever difficulties arose came from the way the scenes were worked out by the cast. Brando began to make his voice heard as the work developed.

In one scene, for example, he felt that Eva Marie Saint was not reacting to him with the viciousness that the situation demanded. Just before shooting began, he started to goad and tease her unmercifully. By the time the cameras rolled she was worked up to a near frenzy.

"I came at him screaming, clawing, and kicking," the petite and otherwise ladylike star said later. "I really wanted to kill him. It was exactly what he had wanted, and after it was over he doubled up with laughter."

Another scene that bothered Brando was the famous one that takes place in a taxi with Rod Steiger, who plays Brando's brother. "Oh, Charlie, Charlie," Terry says, "you didn't understand. I coulda had class . . . I coulda been somebody—instead of a bum—which is what I am." Seven takes of the scene were made. And though Steiger was moved to tears, Brando was never really satisfied. When he saw the scene later in the screening room, he reportedly thought it was so terrible that he walked out without saying a word to Kazan.

There were other things that evidently bothered

Brando about the film. Though it was a crusading effort, the exposé was hung on a formula good-girl-saves-bad-boy plot. Basically the story of a former small-time fighter who is used by corrupt labor leaders on the docks, the film never really gets down to examining the power structure that made conditions on the waterfront possible. The shadowy figure of a "Mr. Big" appears briefly, but the film never clarifies whether he is a political figure, a labor leader, or a shipping company executive. Terry Malloy (Brando) learns that his unwitting complicity with the labor racketeers has been responsible for the death of the brother of Edie Doyle (Eva Marie Saint). After Terry's own brother (Steiger) is killed by the Mob, his girl helps him to see the light, and he becomes a witness for the state at a crime commission inquiry. Afterward, he is branded a "canary" and denied the right to work on the docks. This results in a brutal fight with the labor boss (Lee J. Cobb), from which Terry emerges victorious. He wins the right to work, which supposedly presages the downfall of the corrupt union boss and the end of the union's stranglehold on the dockworkers.

Despite the shortcomings of the plot, *On the Waterfront* was an instantaneous success when it opened in July, 1954. *Life* gave Eva Marie Saint a cover for her work and called the film a magnificent picture. *Time* found it a "shrewd piece of screen journalism in the grand manner of *Public Enemy*." John McCarten in the *New Yorker* said it was "good, tough stuff."

Saint, Steiger, Malden, and Cobb all won high praise for their work. But the greatest kudos were reserved by almost all critics for Brando's portrayal of Terry Malloy. A. H. Weiler wrote in the *New York Times:* "Marlon Brando's Terry Malloy is a shatteringly poignant portrait of an amoral, confused, illiterate citizen of the lower depths." Walter Knight in the *Saturday Review* commented: "Brando's half-articulate hoodlum is developed with an eloquence of gesture and subtlety of inflection that sets a new high for film acting." McCarten predicted, "No actor this year is going to match Mr. Brando's portrayal." And even *Time,* which had taken to making snide remarks about the star, had to admit, "It is a massive performance."

The film quickly captured top honors both at home and abroad. Crowther and Knight named it in their top-ten lists. *Waterfront* won the Best Picture of the Year Award from the New York Film Critics Circle and the Page One Award of the New York Newspaper Guild.

In Dublin, where critics from all over the world gathered to view the film, the Roman Catholic Movie Office gave *On the Waterfront* its Grand Prix. Italian critics presented Brando with a Gold Cup Award and called the film the "first Italian movie made in America." And in England Brando won both the Best Foreign Actor Award of the British Film Academy and a similar honor presented by *Picturegoer Magazine.*

But what about the Academy Awards? Brando and the picture were up against some tough competition. Bing Crosby had done an outstanding job in his first dramatic role in *The Country Girl.* Crosby, who had already won an Oscar, was a sentimental favorite. And *The Country Girl,* written by Clifford Odets and co-starring Grace Kelly, looked like a possible winner of the award for the best film.

To the great credit of the judges, artistry won over sentiment in 1954. Brando could not be denied his Oscar. And carrying the whole *On the Waterfront* slate to victory, his little golden statue generated others for Eva Marie Saint (Best Supporting Actress), Elia Kazan (Best Direction), Budd Schulberg (Best Screenplay),

Boris Kaufman (Best Cinematography), and Sam ("S. P. Eagle") Spiegel (Best Motion Picture).

On Academy Award night Spiegel was so nervous that he couldn't even enter the theater where the festivities were being held. The officials, too, were a bit uneasy. How was Brando going to react? Suppose he turned up in a torn T-shirt and jeans? But all fears were allayed when Brando arrived in an immaculate black-tie-and-tux, looking cool and calm. He tried to persuade Spiegel to join him as he entered, but the producer shook off the star and continued to pace around the lobby.

Finally, when the jittery producer heard Brando's name over the loudspeaker, followed by a great roar, he poked his head inside the door. Brando had moved smoothly, catlike, up to the stage. A hush fell over the audience. Suppose he told them to stuff it?

But Brando simply smiled briefly, looking a bit shy. Then he said, "This is a wonderful moment and a rare one . . . and I'm certainly grateful."

That was it—short and sweet. Brando turned on his heel and marched back to the audience.

Later, he was asked to pose for the usual pictures of the Best Actor kissing the Best Actress. Grace Kelly had scored for her role in *The Country Girl*, and Brando politely bussed her on the cheek. Everything seemed to be going smoothly. But then he finally spoke up regarding the effects of the Awards on an actor.

"There is such a terrible competition," he explained to a reporter, "and a feeling about having to win, that you lose sight of the real objective. You get the feeling you're going to Devil's Island to get your ears chopped off."

Certain members of the Hollywood establishment at the time were interested in pinning Brando's ears back, if not chopping them off. In early 1954 Twentieth

Century-Fox sued Brando for $2 million, claiming that the star was guilty of breach of contract. Brando was in New York at the time the summons was served. Though he normally didn't open his door to strangers, he was tricked by the intrepid court officer, who told him that he had a telegram about an Academy Award.

The suit resulted from Brando's eventual refusal to do *The Egyptian,* which he later called a "camel opera." He tried everything to get out of the contract, and his psychiatrist even stated that he was emotionally too upset to join the cast.

Finally, a compromise was reached. The studio dropped the suit, and Brando agreed to do a different historical romance for Twentieth. At least this one wouldn't have fifty thousand camels stomping around the set. Nevertheless, the incident led to bitter feelings between the star and the studio and alerted other producers that Brando simply would not accept material he disliked without a fight. As one of the leading powers at Twentieth said, "The only good thing I can say about that twerp is that he doesn't like marijuana."

Brando had other troubles in 1954. Some of them concerned women. He had been dating such stars as Pier Angeli, Susan Cabot, and Rita Moreno. He and Moreno had many things in common—from a mutual love of bongos to similar outlooks on Hollywood and life. For a while it looked as though the relationship might become permanent. But then she talked to the press about it—a cardinal sin in Brando's book—and he dropped her. Shortly afterward, there were rumors that Moreno had attempted suicide over the breakup.

Then there was the effect of the Oscar. Brando was the youngest actor in the history of the Academy to win the Best Actor Award. He had become a superstar, but the heightened fame only brought added intrusions into his personal life and placed additional demands on his career. So when he glanced at the miniature golden statue, it must have been with mixed emotions.

6.

Packaging Problems

BRANDO has repeatedly asserted that an actor, whether newcomer, star, or superstar, is nothing more than a product to be foisted on a gullible public. In the years that followed Brando's Oscar-winning performance in *Waterfront,* filmdom was to experience considerable difficulty packaging its most exciting product. Several approaches were considered: the romantic lead, the eternal bad boy, the heavy, and so forth. But there was something about Brando that made such plans untenable. Not only did he make it clear that he was through with rebel roles and would refuse to waste his talent playing historical superheroes, what was worse, he just didn't seem to fit any of the neat Hollywood categories.

Pauline Kael wrote, "When we see him on the screen, we know he is too big for the role." Calling Brando a "Byronic Dead End Kid," she claimed that neither the stage nor the screen had any really worthwhile roles to offer him after *On the Waterfront.* As a result, she maintained, his best subsequent work is really only self-parody.

Kael's assessment seems a bit extreme since it overlooks a number of brilliant roles created by Brando after winning the Oscar. Nonetheless, her article underscores the dilemma facing the studio heads after the 1954 Academy Awards. What were they going to do with Brando?

Part of the problem was that the star himself was changing during this time. At one press conference he would turn up looking like the wrath of God; at another he would be neatly dressed in a pinstriped suit and tie. On one occasion he would discuss his plans for a trip to the Far East; in his next interview he would state that travel had lost all its zest for him. It wasn't surprising that Hollywood was confused about who he was and what he was.

The years 1954 and 1955 thus were bad for Brando. His parents often visited his aunt and uncle in the Los Angeles area during that period. His oldest sister, Jocelyn, was around, too, having come to Hollywood in 1953 to work in *The Big Heat* and *China Venture.* So it seemed that family ties were being reestablished.

But in early spring, 1954, everything seemed to come apart. Dodie Brando suddenly became ill while visiting in California. She was rushed to Huntington Memorial Hospital in Pasadena, where she died on March 31.

It was a great loss, not only to Brando and the family, but to all those who knew the sensitive, talented woman. Rufus Bastian, former art director at Gimbels in New York, said, "She was one of the most wonderful, liberal, open-minded women I've ever known." And

Stella Adler characterized Brando's mother as a "very heavenly, beautiful, lost, girlish creature."

The whole Brando family seemed lost without Dodie. For years she had provided the direction that guided the lives of her children and the fortunes of her family. Those who knew the family well wondered how they would manage without her.

In addition, Brando was having other problems. For a lark he told a gossip columnist that he was secretly engaged to Denise Darcel, the French actress who had come to Hollywood in 1947. When Darcel threatened to sue the paper that ran the story, the enraged reporter confronted Brando. Brando calmly advised him that he thought the newsman was too intelligent to believe such a ridiculous story.

The incident didn't do much to improve his already strained relationship with the press. And when Brando told reporters in the fall of 1954 that he was about to marry Josane Mariani-Berenger, the stepdaughter of a French fisherman, it is perhaps not surprising that they thought he was again making them the butt of his own private joke.

Brando had met Josane earlier that year at a party in the home of Stella Adler. According to her subsequent statements, Josane was only seventeen at the time. She had been an artist's model in France before becoming a live-in maid and nanny for a wealthy New York family. She was dark (a prerequisite for Brando, who never seemed attracted to blonds), shy, and wistfully unspoiled. She stood out from the rest of the people at the party, and Brando and she danced all night, rarely talking. Josane had a certain gamin quality and a streak of Gallic wit that Brando must have found irresistible. She also seemed totally unimpressed by the fact that he was a big star. Perhaps that fact more than anything else attracted him. He asked to see her the following day.

There followed a brief but intense romance, which Brando managed to keep hidden from the press. Josane recalled later that Brando often went to great trouble so that he would not be recognized on the street, transforming himself before her eyes with elaborate makeup. According to Josane, the relationship prospered, and one day Brando marched in to Josane's employers, spoke with them in hushed tones, and told Josane to pack her things. Supposedly, she left without a moment's hesitation and moved into Brando's studio apartment.

Though the affair never became public knowledge, it evidently began to trouble both of them. Seemingly, Brando was still unable to make any lasting commitment to a woman. Josane, though deeply in love with him, found his periods of depression and uncertainty puzzling and destructive. Finally, after months of mutual apprehension and confusion about their true feelings, it was decided that Josane would return to her home in the south of France.

We have only Josane's version of what happened subsequently. According to her, she languished in her home in Bandol, near the French Riviera. Brando wrote regularly for a time, and then his letters stopped. One day Josane was surprised to receive a telegram from Brando, asking her to come to Paris where he was vacationing.

She raced to meet him and he told her that he wanted to return to Bandol with her to meet her parents. They left Paris after a few days and drew crowds whenever they appeared in public.

Brando still seemed uncertain of his plans. But finally he asked Josane's stepfather for her hand in marriage and called a press conference.

It was at this press conference that he made his engagement to Josane official, stating that they would be married the following year. According to Josane, the announcement was followed immediately by feelings of doubt on Brando's part. She later stated that he implied that she was using him, that he had been tricked into proposing. A few days after the press conference, he left for Italy to think things over.

When Brando returned to Josane's home, he asked her to come to America with him. He still seemed uncertain about when, if ever, they would become man and wife. But perhaps he felt that they could work out their problems on the voyage home. In any case, Josane agreed.

They met reporters when they docked in New York in October, 1954. Brando was nattily attired in a suit and raffish Tyrolean hat. Josane smiled shyly in the background, refusing to speak to the gathering of newsmen on the dock.

Brando reportedly told the skeptical press, "This is no joke, no publicity stunt. I really intend to marry the girl."

The reporters pressed him for a date.

"We had planned to set the date for this winter, but we may be changing that," Brando was quoted as saying. "If everything works out it might be much sooner . . . perhaps in a few weeks."

"How do French girls compare with American girls?" one interviewer goaded him.

"I don't see what nationality has to do with choosing a wife," he replied.

That was the last the press heard about Brando's impending marriage to Josane Mariani-Berenger. When reporters questioned him later, he put them off with vague answers.

The two continued to be close, at least for a time. Josane followed Brando to Hollywood, where she made the rounds of the studios in an attempt to break into pictures. But no one was impressed. As one producer said, "Who the hell cares if she's Marlon Brando's girl friend? What difference does that make?" The only work Josane could find was some nude modeling, and a few photos of her turned up in a girlie magazine. After a few months of looking for more challenging work and failing to find it, she finally set sail again for France.

Josane refused to make any statement to the press upon her departure. Later, after she had married a hometown childhood sweetheart and become a mother, she reflected, "Marlon is too independent to accept the discipline of marriage." Nevertheless, Josane and Brando remained on fairly friendly terms. When Brando was near the Riviera, he would sometimes stop in to see her and dandle her child on his knee.

In the midst of his affair with Josane after finishing his work on *Waterfront,* Brando received a phone call from Elia Kazan about an important role. Kazan reportedly told Brando that he wanted him for the young son in *East of Eden*—the Steinbeck novel that the author was adapting for the screen. But Brando apparently felt he was a bit old for the part—he was over thirty. Kazan tried to brush aside the objections, telling Brando that the studio and Steinbeck really wanted him.

Finally, Brando advised his friend that he would have to disappoint him. He had a commitment at Twentieth, and there was no way out of it. In just a few weeks he was supposed to leave for Paris. But he asked Kazan who else he and the studio had in mind for the part.

Kazan didn't hedge. He told Brando they were thinking of James Dean. Reportedly Brando wished him good luck.

Brando evidently had reservations about Dean. The two had met briefly in New York sometime around 1951 when Dean was studying at the Actors Studio. They met again when Dean was appearing in *The Immoralist* on Broadway. Almost seven years younger than Brando, Dean idolized the older star and used Brando as a model for both his acting style and his personal behavior. When Dean came to Hollywood, he aped Brando's slovenly dress, his mannerisms, and his attitude toward the press and the Hollywood establishment.

Brando reportedly found Dean's imitation of him more embarrassing than flattering. In a way it must have been like having the excesses of his youth constantly thrown in his face. In addition, Dean took to calling Brando at all hours of the night and day. The younger actor attempted to arrange meetings and dogged Brando's steps at his favorite places of relaxation.

On two occasions the stars met at studio gatherings in Hollywood. One such encounter took place at the home of Eva Marie Saint, where Brando had shown up with Josane. Josane later said that Dean cornered Brando and wouldn't leave him alone until Brando granted him a private interview. Brando took the younger actor into a room. When the two emerged, after half an hour, Brando told Josane, "That boy is really sick; he needs help."

Evidently, Dean did not take whatever advice Brando gave him. The following year they met again at a party for Sammy Davis, Jr., given by singer Ella Logan. Brando was sporting a neat business suit; Dean had on his usual disheveled outfit. Again Brando listened as Dean poured out his troubles and anxieties. Finally, Brando gave him the name of a psychiatrist and extracted the promise that Dean would seek help.

According to certain sources, Dean made good on this

score. Friends noted that his behavior gradually became less self-destructive.

Nevertheless, he continued to simulate Brando's acting technique. Dean was hailed as a "new Brando" in the publicity releases that preceded *East of Eden.* It seemed to many critics that Kazan had merely transformed Dean into a carbon copy of the star he originally had wanted for his picture.

Crowther complained in his appraisal of *East of Eden,* "Never have we seen a performer so clearly follow another's style. Mr. Kazan should be spanked for allowing him to do such a sophomoric thing."

Brando said, "Jim and I worked together at the Actors Studio in New York, and I have great respect for his talents. However, in *East of Eden* he seems to be wearing my last year's wardrobe and using my last year's talent."

Twentieth Century-Fox had fixed ideas on how to exploit Brando's "this year's talent." The role the studio offered Brando was no less than that of Napoleon.

Brando was forced to star in *Desiree* as part of the compromise he had made with the studio when Twentieth sued him for breach of contract over *The Egyptian.* After he'd finished with *Waterfront,* Twentieth was threatening to sue again if Brando delayed any longer. Brando had no alternative; he accepted his fate and proceeded to throw himself into the role. He was to get a reported $150,000 for his efforts.

Desiree was based on a best-seller by Annemarie Selinko. It chronicled a love affair between the Little Corporal and one of his generals' wives who later became the Queen of Sweden. Lacking any real drama, the picture achieved whatever success it did through a series of stunning tableaux that told the story of Napoleon's career.

No expense was spared in making the film as historically accurate as possible. Uniforms of the emperor and his staff were copied from existing historical models. The costume designers even went so far as to make castings of the original uniform buttons in the interests of authenticity. To give the impression that Brando's feet were as small as Napoleon's, special thin-leather boots were constructed.

The cast was formidable. The English star Jean Simmons played Désirée. The regal Merle Oberon was cast as Josephine. The other players included Michael Rennie, Cameron Mitchell, Cathleen Nesbitt, and Carolyn Jones.

Brando read all the historical material he could find on Napoleon. He developed a quasi-English accent, which some reviewers later said resembled that of Claude Rains. And to keep the image of the would-be world conqueror constantly before him, Brando tacked up a reproduction of a famous portrait of Napoleon in his dressing room.

Studio executive Darryl F. Zanuck, Twentieth's big boss, was satisfied with the picture, calling Brando's performance "great"; the star was less enthusiastic. After the picture was completed, he told one columnist, "Most of the time, I just let the makeup play the part." Later, he said he had tried to get some humor into the part but felt he had failed and consequently found the picture depressing.

The critics didn't all share his feelings. Many found it a typical piece of historical Hollywood puffery, but more were impressed with Brando's acting.

The *New Yorker* found him an "understanding Napoleon," while the *Saturday Review* said that Brando turned in an "interesting performance that shows matchless tension and presence." *Commonweal* stated that the

"new and subdued Brando" was "quite effective."
Others were less impressed. Crowther carped, "Marlon
Brando's Napoleon is just a fancy (and sometimes fatu-
ous) facade." And *Time,* though it featured a picture of
the star—complete with the famous Napoleonic fore-
lock—on its cover, titled its review of the film "Too
Big for His Blue Jeans?" and quipped, "His nose runs
down his face like melted ice cream."

With the cacophony of mixed notices ringing in his
ears, Brando told the press that he was going on a two-
year trip around the world. His dream, he told one interviewer, was to find some island paradise where he could
concern himself with eating, sleeping, and procreation.
On other occasions he said that he was going to join his
father, who was managing his ranch in Nebraska.

Neither the world tour nor the quiet vacation on his
Nebraska acreage became reality during 1955. And it
would take a few more years for his dream of an iso-
lated Eden to come true.

Instead, Brando became interested in another atypi-
cal, offbeat role. He seemingly thought that it might be
fun to try his luck and test his talent as a song-and-
dance man in *Guys and Dolls,* MGM's $5 million adapta-
tion of the Damon Runyon classic.

Brando as a musical comedy star? The critics and
public scoffed—but they also were intrigued. What the
devil was happening to Brando? First Napoleon and
then Sky Masterson.

Brando evidently had decided to stop biting the hand
that fed him. Recalling this period of his life, when he
kept talking about giving up acting and pursuing other
interests, he later said, "This all showed my disappointment with myself. I kept talking about quitting and
pursuing other interests. But how was I to pursue them
if I didn't know what they were?"

So Brando began to make as much money as possible while still remaining independent, an outsider.

Guys and Dolls provided him with an excellent vehicle for realizing at least the financial goals of his new course of action. Not only did he obtain a $200,000 salary for his role, he demanded—and was given—certain rights regarding script approval.

The cast gathered for the production promised an outstanding film. Brando's friend Mankiewicz was to direct. Sam Goldwyn, who had left MGM in 1924, was returning to his old studio to produce the picture. And that meant no money would be spared to make the film a box-office bonanza.

The cast included Frank Sinatra as Nathan Detroit. Jean Simmons was again the apple of Brando's eye—this time as Sarah Brown, the Salvation Army reformer. Reenacting the roles they had created for the Broadway production, which had tallied 1,200 performances and been a gold mine for its backers, were Vivian Blaine and Stubby Kaye. The Goldwyn Girls completed the ensemble.

When Brando was asked why the role appealed to him, he stated that he wanted to do something bright—something *"yellow."* Up to this time the brightest thing he'd done was "red—red, brown, gray, down to black."

Brando had this to say about his singing ability: "I'm stretching out in this part. Up to this time the only singing I've done has been in the bathtub. But my voice coach tells me I'll be quite a dramatic tenor."

Of course, there was also the question of whether he could dance. Brando had studied dancing with Kathryn Dunham a few years earlier, but he had not been trained for the kind of tricky hoofing he would have to do in *Guys and Dolls.*

Helping Brando—and Jean Simmons, who also had

never danced before—was Michael Kidd, who had been the dance director of the Broadway production. After he had worked with the stars for a few weeks, Kidd told *Dance* magazine, "Working with them has been a pleasure. Although both [Brando and Simmons] had a minimum of training, they're both musical, gifted, and love to dance."

Kidd had only one objection to working with Brando. At the time, the star had just stopped smoking. Perhaps to make up for his loss of oral gratification, he had taken to chewing whole packages of gum at a time. Brando chomped away during the dance sequences, snapped his gum unconsciously while Kidd was giving directions, and burst bubbles all over his fresh makeup. Finally, Kidd could stand it no longer. He obtained a large tin can on which he painted the legend "Brando's Gum Here!" A stagehand followed Brando around the set with the can, making sure that the actor deposited the offensive gum before the cameras rolled.

Work on the film began in April, 1955, and ended three months later. When *Guys and Dolls* opened in November of that year, several thousand people crowded around the New York theater. Fans almost carried Brando off when he stepped from his car.

The critics were less impressed. Crowther felt that the film lacked the spice and drive of the stage offering. And he found the performances of Brando and Sinatra disappointing. "Brando is a shade too much like a Mr. Big in a gangster film," he wrote, "and Sinatra is too serene." Nevertheless, Crowther named *Guys and Dolls* among his top twenty films for the year.

Others echoed Crowther's feelings. Robert Hatch wrote in the *Nation* that Brando was a "sheepish song and dance man." McCarten, on the other hand, commented that Brando was a convincing gambler, even though he sang "through a rather unwieldy set of sinuses." Arthur Knight, concentrating on the terpsichorean ability of the star, noted in *Dance:* "Brando, entering after the dance [the "Lady Luck" number], conveys more of its mood through his own intensity and sinuous rhythmic movement than the dance itself."

Well, so much for musical comedy. There hadn't been a whisper about an Award nomination for his performance in *Desiree,* and the same was true for his work in *Guys and Dolls.* With a new-found sense of detachment about his career, Brando seemed satisfied with and even amused by his situation. He was earning huge sums to enlarge his talent, test his wings.

Studio heads were less jovial. The way the fans were responding to Brando at the box office proved that he had tremendous drawing power. But there was still the problem of packaging. What kind of picture would show Brando to best advantage and bring in maximum returns?

Even more troubling than the packaging problem was Brando's announcement, after finishing *Guys and Dolls,* that he and his father were setting up their own company to produce films. Named after Brando's great-grandfather, Pennebaker Productions was soon incorporated. Marlon, Sr., served as president and treasurer; Marlon, Jr., was first vice-president; Walter Seltzer was second vice-president; and Robin Marbin filled the post of secretary. According to the new company's first vice-president, the primary purpose of the organization was to make worthwhile films. But the studios realized that Brando would also be taking a bigger slice of the profits if he starred in films that his company produced.

In this respect Brando was in the advance guard of a movement that was to sweep through the movie industry in the decades that followed. The advent of television had put the major studios in a financial bind. During the late forties and early fifties the studios began to take a new look at some of their big stars. A lot of contracts were not renewed, and executives were wary of tying up potential new stars with long-term agreements. This development led to one-picture arrangements, which actors such as Brando, Clift, and others found quite advantageous. But a Pandora's Box had been opened. Brando and other stars, such as John Wayne, Alan Ladd, and Gregory Peck, soon realized that it would be still more lucrative for them to set up their own production companies, borrowing money from the studios in return for distribution rights. They could then walk off with the lion's share of the profits plus ownership of their own films in perpetuity.

Brando's new company had not yet decided on its first film. Brando was looking around for something suitable. In fact, shortly after Pennebaker Productions was incorporated, he hired a staff of readers to scout worthwhile material.

While Brando was busy with his new company, he lost out on the role of Frankie Machine, the drug addict in Nelson Algren's *The Man with the Golden Arm.* Otto Preminger was about to make the film version, and he sent the first forty pages of the script simultaneously to the agents of Brando and Sinatra. It is not known whether Brando ever got a chance to consider the part. The day after the script had been sent to Sinatra's agent, Preminger received a call advising him that the singer-turned-actor wanted the part. Preminger was a bit surprised that Sinatra had made a decision without seeing the rest of the script, but he quickly signed Sinatra to a contract.

It would have been interesting to see what Brando could have done with the part. Perhaps his reluctance to respond with the alacrity of Sinatra was due to the fact that Frankie Machine was too "dark," that he wanted to stay with the "yellows." In any case, his next role was a bright one. Another nutty offer came in from MGM. The studio wanted Brando to play the part that David Wayne had made famous on Broadway in *The Teahouse of the August Moon.* Brando would have to transform himself from rebel to Okinawan houseboy.

The idea appealed to Brando for several reasons. First, there was the money: he would receive his best salary ever for his efforts. Second, the picture would provide him with a free ride to the Orient—a place that had been in the back of his mind for years. In addition, he looked forward to the challenge of the role and the opportunity to work with director Daniel Mann, who had developed a good reputation among serious film-goers for his efforts in *Come Back, Little Sheba* and *The Rose Tattoo.*

The role of Sakini was not without problems for Brando. It took more than an hour and a half every morning to transform himself into an Oriental. This was reportedly accomplished by filling in his tear ducts with rubber and fitting him with a black, straight-haired wig.

A greater task was shedding the excess weight that he had begun to acquire. Brando was carrying 180 pounds on his five-foot-ten-inch frame and was beginning to look decidedly pudgy. Doubtless the fact that he had quit smoking was partially responsible for his weight problem. As with many former smokers, food began to taste much better to him. And the temptations of the exotic dishes of Japan, where the film was shot, probably proved to be too much. He was forced to go on a strict diet. Characteristically, Brando threw himself into the role, trying to make his performance as realistic as possible. He wanted to be able to speak English like a native Okinawan, so he decided to learn Japanese.

Brando explained his method to an interviewer:

"I had to learn the language by rote, copying the inflections. I have no feelings for the words. I'm flying blind on that score. To most Americans, Japanese is a series of unfamiliar sounds without any intonation or rhythm within their experience. I played my lines as spoken by a native on a tape recorder. My teacher and I would repeat over and over again the same line until I could imitate him."

Brando learned quickly that the Japanese cannot easily pronounce *f, l,* or *r.* But he felt that he would be nearly unintelligible to American audiences if he used this knowledge in his role. So he edited as he went along, fumbling with the "difficult" consonants only occasionally.

Brando was impressed with the ability of the Japanese actors in the cast—as well as with their sometimes mercurial behavior.

"Japanese actors responded like fine artists, sensitive and imaginative," he observed. "Contrary to what I'd heard about Orientals being tranquil, I found them as emotional as Italians."

The film, which centers around the trials of an American army captain whose mission is to Americanize occupied Okinawa, had some initial production problems. The original plan had been to shoot substantial portions in Japan. But Louis Calhern, one of the principals, died as filming began. By the time Paul Ford was available to replace Calhern, the shooting was threatened by Japan's rainy season. The cast was forced to return to Hollywood.

Despite Brando's hard work, the critics for the most part were hostile. Crowther felt that director Mann had broadened the farce to such an extent that it resembled Martin-and-Lewis slapstick. "Brando," he wrote, "goes his merry way making gestures with his hands and garbling verbiage with sublime and almost reckless unconcern for any pretense of initiating a plausible or warm character. Beneath a dark stain, bad eye makeup, and a wig of shiny black hair, you see Mr. Brando enjoying a romp in his own little show."

Alpert in the *Saturday Review* contended that good plays don't always make good movies. He found Brando "virtually wasted" in the production. The *New Yorker* critic, McCarten, said that Brando looked like an American boy trying to play Fu Manchu. On the other hand, Pauline Kael characterized Brando's performance as "hilarious." But the picture didn't make anyone's list of the top films of 1956, and Brando didn't win any honors for his role.

After the critical disaster of *Teahouse,* the star perhaps realized that he was going to need more control over his future pictures if he was going to protect his reputation. Thus, when Joshua Logan first approached him with the script for *Sayonara,* Brando turned it down flat.

Logan, coming from Broadway with a good reputation as a producer, had received critical acclaim for his direction of Hollywood's *Picnic* and *Bus Stop.* Brando may have thought that it might be interesting to work with Logan, but he had serious reservations about the script. The initial adaptation of what one critic called "James Michener's Japanese baloney" apparently struck Brando as too simplistic and sentimental. The hero seemed like an updated Rover Boy. But Brando also saw a potential message about racial tolerance in the story of the relationships between occupying military personnel and their Japanese loves.

Logan was persistent in his efforts to persuade Brando to play the lead, and Brando found the idea of returning to Japan attractive. The star finally agreed to talk over his objections with the director.

Brando pointed out that he didn't like the script for a variety of reasons. The character of the American woman was a stereotype; there was nothing to the role of Major Gruver for which he was being sought. In addition, he felt that in order to underscore the message of racial tolerance, the Japanese as well as the Americans should be shown to be guilty of racial prejudice and that he should marry the Japanese girl in the end. Finally, he announced that he wanted his contract to give him certain rights concerning the script.

Even though Logan urged him to rewrite any parts of the script he didn't like, assuring Brando he could get approval from the studio, the star still didn't seem sold on the idea. He took the script, thought it over, then went back for another meeting with Logan. At this time, he reportedly advised the director that he wanted 10 percent of the gross. Again, Logan seemed agreeable, and again Brando backed off.

It wasn't till a few days later that Logan finally got word from the star. Reportedly Brando told Logan that what had decided him was the way Logan had removed some dead leaves from one of his houseplants. Evidently he sensed some inner quality of sensitivity in the director that appealed to him.

Logan wasn't sure at the time whether the explanation was a put-on. And after he'd worked with the star for a few weeks, he began to wonder whether he had made the right decision in seeking out Brando. The star, back in a country that was becoming almost a second home to him, was in a rare mood, and his high spirits bubbled over on the set.

Logan later told the press, "He was maliciously determined to upset any note of sobriety on the set. He had a pin hidden somewhere, perhaps in his lapel, that he used to prick any semblance of law and order."

The director went on to describe the time that his leading actor appeared on location with his arm in a sling, saying that he had dislocated his shoulder. Logan, the cast, and the crew started to pack up.

Brando told the director that he could still speak his lines. Everything will be okay, he said, as long as he didn't have to do something like this. He then removed the supposedly injured arm from the sling, raised it high, and brought it down with force into his other hand. Everyone just stood around dumbfounded till he began laughing hysterically. Logan seemed far from amused.

Logan had other difficulties both before and after the picture got under way. There was the Japanese impresario who had promised to furnish authentic Geisha girls, Kabuki and Noh actors, and an all-girl band. As negotiations proceeded, the price for obtaining the performers kept getting higher and higher. Finally, it reached astronomical proportions, and the idea had to be dropped.

The air force provided another stumbling block. Logan needed the military's cooperation since part of the film was to be shot on an air force base in Japan. But the brass in Washington didn't care for some of the implications they found in the script. For example, the film as first written implied that men about to take Japanese wives found themselves being shipped home. Eventually, the air force had its way. The implication was cut from the movie, and Logan obtained rights to use the government-owned location for shooting.

Finally, there was the question of Brando's leading lady. Logan had hoped to get Audrey Hepburn to play opposite Brando as the Japanese girl, but she couldn't break a prior commitment. So the director sponsored a beauty contest in Japan in hopes of discovering a female lead, but none of the contestants was suitable. He then decided to search for an Oriental-American who might fit the bill, eventually coming up with Miiko Taka, a California nisei girl who had never acted before.

Brando, meanwhile, was having his own problems. Told to lose 20 pounds for the role, he had gained almost that many and was approaching 200. He finally went back to smoking, and that helped a bit.

There was also the question of Brando's accent. Logan had bought the idea that Brando had suggested of making Major Gruver the scion of a Southern family. But it was going to take work to make Brando's speech believable. Out came the star's trusty tape recorder again. Working with speech coach Carlo Fiori, Brando finally got his drawl down pat. Even Logan, a Southerner himself, was impressed. He told friends, "Marlon's the most authentic corn-fed Southern gentleman I have seen outside of the real ones I knew as a boy."

The relationship between the director and star was an unusual one. Logan had great respect for Brando's intuitive abilities, and he gave the star free rein in developing his character. "I've never worked with such an inventive, creative actor," he wrote later. "Whenever he came up with something new, I wanted those creative moments recorded. And a lot of them are in the picture."

Brando, for his part, probably enjoyed the freedom and was honored by the respect afforded him. But then he seemed to wonder if Logan knew what he was doing. Brando experimented—grimacing, rolling his eyes, sitting when he should have been standing, laughing when he should have been solemn—and Logan seemed to think that it was all wonderful. In view of some of the outlandish things he did, Brando couldn't believe his ears when he heard the director say, "Great! Print it!"

Brando as Terry Malloy in **On the Waterfront**, the role that won him his Oscar for Best Actor of 1954. *(Photo Memory Shop)*

(Above) Director Elia Kazan and
his stars Brando and Vivien Leigh
ponder the famous rape scene in
the movie version of **Streetcar**.
Kazan's direction was later
toned-down through editing to
avoid a "condemned" rating.
(Photo Memory Shop)

(Above left) To help the cause of
Jewish refugees and promote a new
Jewish state, Brando joined
veterans Paul Muni and Ceilia Adler
in the Broadway production of Ben
Hecht's **A Flag Is Born**. *(Photo
Movie Memorabilia)*

(Left) With or without the
characteristic ripped T-shirt,
Brando made an immediate impact
on Broadway with his portrayal of
Stanley Kowalski in **A Streetcar
Named Desire**. *(Photo Movie
Memorabilia)*

(Below) Brando made his screen debut as the embittered paraplegic veteran in Stanley Kramer's **The Men** and won wide critical acclaim. Everett Sloane is shown assisting the new star in the tense wedding scene in which he marries Teresa Wright.

"Cry havoc! And let slip the dogs of war!"
Brando astounded critics by his ability to
master Shakespeare's verse in Joseph
Mankiewicz's **Julius Caesar.** His performance
brought him another nomination for best
actor of the year. *(Photo Movie Memorabilia)*

Caesar (Louis Calhern) and Mark Antony (Brando) relax on set following
the assassination scene in **Julius Caesar.** *(Photo Memory Shop)*

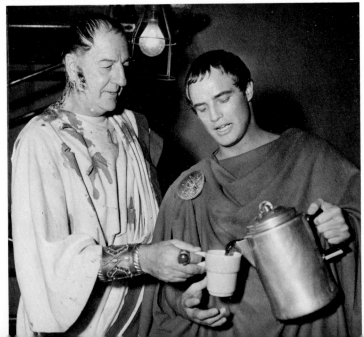

Viva Zapata! teamed Brando and Anthony Quinn as revolutionary Mexican brothers. As the idealistic Zapata, Brando pushed aside medals; as a new box-office sensation, he won his third consecutive Academy Award nomination for the role. *(Photo Memory Shop)*

The characteristic, explosive Brando acting style erupts in a scene from the screen version of **Streetcar**. Kim Hunter tries to deal with her enraged husband as Vivien Leigh retreats in terror. *(Photo Movie Memorabilia)*

Jay C. Flippen as the ineffectual sheriff worries about the fate of his town when rival gangs led by Lee Marvin (left) and Brando roar down its peaceful streets on their cycles in **The Wild One.** *(Photo Movie Memorabilia)*

Karl Malden as a tough waterfront priest and Eva Marie Saint as the working-class "good girl" tend Terry's wounds after the big fight scene with Lee J. Cobb in **On the Waterfront.** *(Photo Movie Memorabilia)*

Best Actor of 1954 busses Best
Actress, Grace Kelly, after
Academy Award presentations.
(Photo Movie Memorabilia)

There were no Oscar nominations for
Brando when he appeared as Napoleon with
Jean Simmons in **Desiree.** He later said that
he let the costume play the role. *(Photo
Movie Memorabilia)*

To prove his versatility, Brando switched to musical comedy in **Guys and Dolls.**
Critics were not impressed, but the public flocked to see the songfest that
included Brando, Jean Simmons, Frank Sinatra, and Vivian Blaine. *(Photo Memory Shop)*

(Above) Brando was chewing tons of gum on the set of **Guys and Dolls** to keep from smoking. Choreographer Michael Kidd (left) devised a special container to keep Brando from walking on-camera while chomping away. *(Photo Memory Shop)*

(Left) Another change of pace for Brando came in **The Teahouse of the August Moon**, in which he played the Okinawan houseboy, Sakini. With the help of his personal makeup man, it took four hours to transform the star from Occidental to Oriental. *(Photo Memory Shop)*

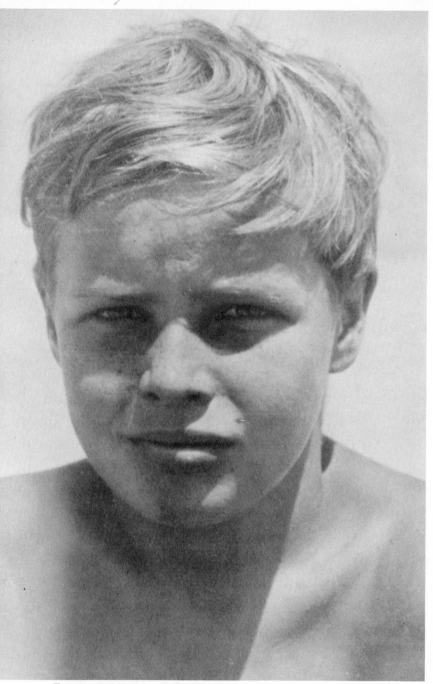
Tow-headed Buddy at the age of 11. *(Photo Culver Pictures)*

Sister Frannie at the time of
her graduation from high
school.

Teen-aged Brando fed the chickens and milked the cow while his
family lived in this huge farmhouse just outside Libertyville, Illinois.

Father, Marlon, Sr., and mother, Dodie,
showed up on location in New York for
the shooting of **On the Waterfront**.
(Photo Movie Memorabilia)

Older sister Jocelyn had just finished filming **The Big Heat**
when she stopped in to see her kid brother on **The Wild
One** set. *(Photo Movie Memorabilia)*

Screen newcomer Red Buttons won an Oscar
as Best Supporting Actor for his role in
Sayonara; but Brando received only a
nomination for Best Actor for his portrayal
of the Southern Major Gruver. *(Photo Memory Shop)*

On a "chopper" again—this time with Maximillian Schell in **The Young Lions**. Brando insisted on script changes that would make his role as a Nazi more sympathetic to underscore the broader anti-nationalistic message of the movie.

Brando dislocated a shoulder showing Karl Malden how to use a bull-whip in **One Eyed Jacks**. Here, Malden shows he learned his lesson well in the picture that was to be Brando's first and only directorial effort. Some critics hailed it as introducing an important new directorial talent. *(Photo Movie Memorabilia)*

(Below) Not even the star-studded cast of Brando, Magnani, and Woodward saved **The Fugitive Kind** from being a box-office disaster. Playwright Tennessee Williams who adapted his play **Orpheus Descending** for the screen was booed by the audience when the film opened in New York. *(Photo Movie Memorabilia)*

(Above) While still acting on Broadway, Brando announced his engagement to Cecilia D'Artuniaga, a publicist born in South America. *(Photo Culver Pictures)*

(Left) Movita, the second Mrs. Brando, when she was a star at Monogram Pictures, circa 1938. *(Photo Culver Pictures)*

(Above) Everyone was surprised when the off-again-on-again romance of Brando and Anna Kashfi ended in a Mr. and Mrs. ceremony. The groom is still sporting blond hair from his role in **The Young Lions**; the bride looked very Indian in her sari despite later disclosures by the press about her nationality. *(Photo Movie Memorabilia)*

Brando with his oldest son, Christian, on way to Santa Monica courthouse in March, 1972, when he won custody of the boy from Anna Kashfi. *(Photo Movie Memorabilia)*

Between scenes of **Mutiny on the Bounty,** Brando and Tarita relax on a Tahitian beach. *(Photo Culver Pictures)*

Always the gentleman, Brando's Fletcher Christian prevents one of his cohorts from attacking the despised Captain Bligh of Trevor Howard in **Mutiny on the Bounty.** The critics and public, expecting a re-run of the Clark Gable portrayal of Christian, were upset by Brando's interpretation of the role. *(Photo Memory Shop)*

As the irrepressible cowboy, Matt, in **The Appaloosa**, Brando infiltrates hostile Mexican territory to reclaim his stolen horse. *(Photo Memory Shop)*

(Above left) Brando and Sophia Loren did their best to
load the ill-fated **A Countess from Hong Kong** with laughs,
but the critics were unimpressed. *(Photo Memory Shop)*

(Below) The man for whom Brando said **he** would work in
a phone booth made a brief (and perhaps his last) screen
appearance in **Countess,** which Chaplin also wrote and
directed. When critics found the legendary master's film old
fashioned, Charlie called them bloody idiots. *(Photo Movie
Memorabilia)*

Brando and David Niven were brothers in **Bedtime Story**, a fast-paced comedy that Brando's Pennebaker Productions made strictly for money. Some called his clowning distasteful; others called him a master farceur. *(Photo Memory Shop)*

The U.S. State Department was concerned about how "ugly" Brando would make **The Ugly American**, which, though set in the mythical land of Sarkhan, was obviously meant as a statement about Vietnam. Critics praised his portrayal of the bumbling diplomat. *(Photo Memory Shop)*

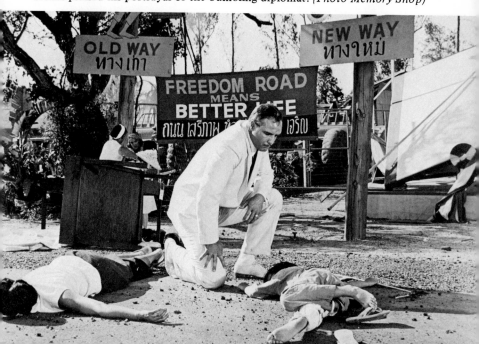

(Right) Brando, playing a Jewish guru, was the only one to gain the favors of sex-object Ewa Aulin in **Candy**, the picture that supposedly couldn't be made. Most critics wished it hadn't. *(Photo Movie Memorabilia)*

(Below) Chow time on the set of **The Chase**. The presence of veterans such as Brando, E. G. Marshall, and Janice Rule plus newcomers Jane Fonda and Robert Redford didn't save the tawdry tale at the box office. *(Photo Memory Shop)*

Top billing in **Reflections in a Golden Eye** went to Elizabeth Taylor; but the critics were most impressed with Brando's portrayal of her husband, the strange Major with homosexual leanings. *(Photo Movie Memorabilia)*

(Above) Lack of publicity probably kept **Burn!**, the story of a black revolution, from being popular with a new generation of filmgoers. Brando, shown here with Evaristo Marquez, played an English agent who betrays the revolutionaries. *(Photo Memory Shop)*

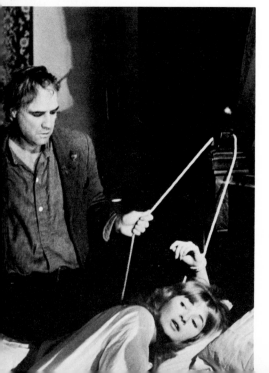

Brando and Stephanie Beachan played the lovers who corrupt two children in **The Nightcomers**. Neither sex nor sadism kept this variation of a Henry James story from bombing with the public. *(Photo Memory Shop)*

The Godfather brought Brando back into the public eye as perhaps the greatest actor of his time. Al Pacino, as the youngest son and heir apparent, had nothing but praise for Brando's reading of the character of Vito Corleone, the aging Don. *(Photo Movie Memorabilia)*

The Godfather ponders the advice of his *consigliori*, played by Robert Duval. A guardian angel must have guided Brando in his decision to seek the role; for the movie immediately set new box-office records and will doubtless replace **Gone with the Wind** as the top money-earner of all time. *(Photo Movie Memorabilia)*

Perhaps the wily Logan felt that the best way to treat an allegedly temperamental actor was to let him have his way. After all, Brando's unsuccessful experiments could all be edited out. Indeed, of the many lines that Brando had rewritten, only about eight remained in the finished product.

Brando was gracious and fun-loving on the set, but after hours he rarely saw the rest of the company. Logan complained that Brando was the most exciting actor he'd met since Garbo—but that he still didn't know anything about him as a person.

Brando confined his socializing to a closed circle of people whom he had brought with him—his father, secretary, personal makeup artist, and a writer who was helping him with a script that he planned to turn into a Pennebaker film.

The distance between Brando and the rest of the people associated with the film evidently didn't affect the finished product. When *Sayonara* opened in New York in December, 1957, the reviews supported Logan's optimistic predictions. McCarten liked Brando's "cornpone and chittlin' accent" and said that it gave an added dimension to the picture. Pauline Kael was lukewarm on the film but praised Brando's efforts. Only *Time,* in its usual manner, was negative on Brando's performance. His accent, the reviewer wrote, sounded as though it had been "strained through Stanislavsky's mustache."

Crowther wrote a favorable review and later named *Sayonara* among the top ten films of the year. "Thanks to the remarkably thought-out and interestingly faceted performance of an American West Point officer by the stellar Marlon Brando," he wrote, "the modern tale of an American's love for a Japanese girl has fascination and meaning."

The critical praise didn't help Brando when Academy

Award night rolled around. Though he had been nominated again for Best Actor, the big picture that year was David Lean's *The Bridge on the River Kwai,* which walked off with honors for Best Motion Picture, Best Direction, and Best Actor (Alec Guinness). But film newcomer Red Buttons and Miyoshi Umeki (a Japanese star) captured the awards for Best Supporting Actor and Best Supporting Actress for their portrayal of *Sayonara's* doomed lovers.

Brando wasn't seen the night the envelopes were opened. He was too busy getting ready to do a film for Pennebaker Productions. Considerably more pragmatic by this time, Brando wanted Pennebaker's first picture to be profitable so that he could develop a nest egg for future efforts. Brando told the press that the film would be a western, that he would star in it, that he was helping to write the script, and that he hoped that it would deliver a message about intolerance (in addition to a good return on his money). Brando probably made a mistake in talking to the press in such detail about the venture. But he was growing more assured and less reporter-shy than he had been in the past.

This development was to have an adverse effect on his image. During the filming of *Sayonara,* Brando had granted an interview to Truman Capote, writing for the *New Yorker.* The writer, often viewed as a lap-dog of the Beautiful People, evidently felt compelled to do a real hatchet job on the outspoken actor. The article that finally appeared, almost a year later, was blatantly contemptuous.

Capote commented slyly on the way the Japanese maids treated Brando in his hotel and meticulously described the disarray of Brando's suite. The questions he put to Brando were designed to make the star appear foolish whichever way he answered. Capote's article insinuated that Brando equated success with making money, that he had failed to live up to the promise of his early career, and that he was intellectually pretentious.

It is difficult to judge just why Capote went out of his way to hurt Brando. Perhaps it was because the outspoken star had attacked the writer's beloved Fat City with its precious Broadway. When Capote asked Brando why he didn't return to the stage, the actor asked why he should since the movies had a greater potential for bringing about social change. Worst of all, Brando asked what was so great about New York.

At any rate, Capote's attack spawned a number of other adverse appraisals of Brando's career and personality over the next few years. Hollis Alpert took the star to task for failing to return to Broadway. Dwight Mac-Donald in *Esquire* attacked Brando for being a pseudointellectual.

The bad press left its mark. But in the troublesome years that were just ahead, the vicious attacks of the press were to be among the least of Brando's problems.

7.

The Most Important Thing

DURING one of the rare interviews in which Brando talked seriously about himself, the star was asked what was most important in his life. Thinking the question over for a few moments, Brando replied slowly, "Love is the only reason for living. It's the most important thing."

The admission surprised those—and there were many—who thought of Brando as a typical Hollywood Don Juan. He had dated both ordinary working girls and some of the most glamorous young starlets of his day. Twice he had announced his intention to marry; yet he was still a bachelor. When he was on location for *Teahouse* and *Sayonara,* rumors had filtered back to the film capital about liaisons with Japanese girls. But whenever the press asked about his intentions, he either refused to discuss his most recent romance or announced that it had cooled.

117

Was this the way a man who placed so much emphasis on love behaved? Perhaps Brando felt that it was the *only* way to protect himself and the women with whom he was involved. When asked why he didn't give the public a break and let them in on his romantic life, Brando responded bitterly, "I don't see how you can expect a person to take sensitive parts of himself and splatter them around like peanut butter."

The reporters and columnists were not impressed. Didn't Brando's behavior really indicate an unwillingness to commit himself? they asked. And didn't his preference for ordinary girls and young starlets indicate a need to feel superior? He probably felt, the columnists hinted, that women were mere playthings to be used and discarded as he saw fit. Nobody called him a male chauvinist pig at the time, but the implication was there.

In fact, Brando's attitude toward women was far in advance of his time. For instance, he told Arlene Dahl that the woman he most admired was Madame Pandit (the former president of the UN General Assembly). The selection evidently surprised Ms. Dahl because Brando went on to explain, "After all, women came to be considered inferior because they weren't physically as strong." But "the inferiority of women is an antiquated idea and a mark of immaturity in the culture that allows it."

Many columnists were miffed about the fact that Brando showed very little interest in the typical all-American girl. In fact, most of his girl friends were not even Americans. Josane, for example, was French; Movita, Mexican. Rita Moreno was born in Puerto Rico; Pier Angeli was a native of Italy; and Cecelia D'Artuniaga (the girl to whom he had announced his engagement in 1948) was from Colombia.

After Brando's work in Japan, his taste seemed to

swing to even more exotic types. Roberta Haynes, whom he dated for a while, had made her mark as a Polynesian beauty in *Return to Paradise* with Gary Cooper. Was Brando anti-American? the columnists asked.

There is no question that Brando had for some time been fascinated by the East. As early as 1948 he was reading Zen philosophy and studying Yoga. And it seems likely that this fascination with the Orient was partially responsible for one of the most unfortunate mistakes of his life.

One day while walking through the studio in 1957, just after Brando had returned from making *Sayonara,* he caught sight of a dark, slender beauty wearing an Indian sari. After making a few inquiries, he discovered that the woman's name was Anna Kashfi. She was reportedly from India and had been discovered the previous year by Edward Dmytryk, who gave her the female lead opposite Spencer Tracy in *The Mountain.* At the time Brando first noticed her, she was working with Jack Lemmon and Glen Ford in *Cowboy.*

At Brando's request, director A. C. Lyles arranged an introduction in the studio commissary at Paramount. There followed an intense, on-again, off-again romance. According to some sources, Brando at first monopolized almost all of Anna's time. They kept to out-of-the-way places in the less fashionable districts of Los Angeles and the beatnik sections of Venice. Sometimes they met in the homes of Brando's friends—such people as Pete Berneis, a free-lance film writer, and George Englund, a producer-director.

Anna and Brando were seen together almost nightly for a few weeks, but few took the relationship seriously, especially when Sam Gilman, the actor who sometimes shared Brando's Benedict Canyon home at this time, reported that the two had broken up and hadn't seen each other for quite some time.

Brando, in any case, had other matters to divert his attention. One of these was the result of his negotiations with Dmytryk. He had been given the script of *The Young Lions* to look over, and Dmytryk and Twentieth Century-Fox wanted a quick answer.

Lions had a lot of potential in Brando's opinion. The fact that Dmytryk was to direct was significant, and the cast was topflight, including such names as Montgomery Clift, Dean Martin, Hope Lange, Barbara Rush, May Britt, and Maximilian Schell. But Brando was not pleased with the script that Irwin Shaw had adapted from his best-selling novel.

The original version was entirely too anti-German in its outlook. Brando felt that it was important to make an antiwar picture, but he didn't like the idea of using the Germans as scapegoats. In his view the horrors of nazism were possible in any country.

Brando suggested that the role of the Nazi officer be rewritten. He thought the character should be more like the rebel in *The Wild One,* who just goes along with the trouble once it gets under way.

Twentieth Century-Fox, judging from the $200,000 salary it was offering Brando, wanted him very badly. The studio finally conceded to Brando's demands on the script and agreed to give him approval rights over certain parts of it.

Brando was enthusiastic about the picture. He told the press, "They say in Hollywood if you want messages you go to Western Union. People are not interested in message pictures, but entertainment. I believe a combination of both is possible and essential, particularly in the international exchange of ideas."

The film followed two American soldiers and a Ger-

man officer from their civilian lives through their involvement in World War II. It provided a showcase for
the contrasting talents of Brando and Montgomery Clift,
considered America's two leading exponents of the
Method school of acting. Fans argued back and forth as
to which of the actors was better and which one had
influenced the other more.

Such arguments were largely academic. The two men
had developed independently, and about the only things
they had in common were their birthplace and the quality of intensity each brought to his roles. Both had entered movies after prior successes on the Broadway stage,
but Clift had never studied at the Actors Studio or any
other studio where Method acting was taught. Instead
he had learned his craft from such seasoned performers
as Thomas Mitchell and Alfred Lunt. The two actors
projected entirely different screen images. Brando's was
a physical, emotional presence; Clift seemed cooler,
more intellectual, with that blank stare of a young bird
that had become his trade-mark.

However, a friendly rivalry developed between the
two stars. This was to be the first and only time they
would appear together, and each was probably determined to turn in the best performance he could.

Brando dyed his hair blond and began practicing a
German accent. Clift, who played an American Jew in
the film, later said that he brought to his part "an
amalgam of all the daily living, loving, and not loving of
my life."

Doubtless it irked Clift that his rival was given top
billing on the picture. But there was little he could do
about it since at the time Brando was a far bigger box-
office attraction. Clift did try to make sure that nothing
undercut the sympathy he felt his role should generate.
On one occasion, when Brando suggested that he should

fall spread-eagle across a barbed-wire fence when Clift killed him at the end of the film, Clift stormed off the set. One observer commented, "When Clift is in a movie, there's only room for one Christ figure."

Ultimately, Brando won higher critical acclaim for his performance than did Clift. Crowther noted, "As it happens, Mr. Brando makes the German much more vital and interesting than Montgomery Clift and Dean Martin make the Americans." Arthur Knight in the *Saturday Review* agreed. Robert Hatch in the *Nation* commented at length on Brando: "He is interesting, as he always is. He can put a unique stamp on any role he plays, doing things with his body and face and voice that are eloquent and seem to imply the creation of a complex character." By contrast, Hatch glossed over Clift's contribution.

Despite its two-and-a-half-hour length, the movie was well received by both the critics and the American public. However, after opening successfully in New York (at a benefit for the Actors Studio attended by Brando, Clift, Elia Kazan, Lee Strasberg, Hope Lange, and other notables), it did run into trouble overseas. Americans were willing to accept the overall antiwar message made possible by Brando's revision of the Nazi character. Such was not the case in Israel, where *Lions* soon ran into problems with the censors.

Israeli censors were hesitant to approve the film because it portrayed Nazis in a sympathetic light. But as Israel was deciding the picture's fate, its traditional enemy, Egypt, banned *The Young Lions.* In the light of Egypt's action, Israel could hardly condemn the film. Ironically, when Israeli censors finally permitted the film to be screened, it drew record crowds in Jerusalem.

An Israeli official explained: "We don't believe a Nazi such as Mr. Brando's ever existed. But we were in a difficult spot. The film had been banned in Egypt because it shows an American Jewish soldier in a very good light. It would have been a bit ironic and ridiculous for us to ban it on the basis it is anti-Jewish."

After finishing the picture, Brando again returned to Hollywood, where he and Sam Gilman (whom Brando had helped to obtain a small part in *Lions*) again set up headquarters in Brando's small house. Gilman didn't see much of his friend, however, since the romance between Brando and Kashfi now moved into high gear.

The tongues of the columnists were clacking, but no one was prepared for what took place in the home of Brando's aunt and uncle in Eagle Rock, California, on October 11, 1957. Early that day Brando was seen rushing in and out of a jewelry shop in nearby Pasadena. Since at the time he was garbed in flowing Hindu robes, it is not surprising that he attracted a mob.

Later, a small group of friends and Brando's family gathered before the Reverend Walter J. Fiscus of North Hollywood's nondenominational Little Brown Church in the Valley. Brando was wearing a dark suit and dark tie; Anna Kashfi, his bride, was clad in an exquisite pale green sari embroidered in gold. It was a short, simple ceremony. Peter Berneis gave the bride away, and Marlon, Sr., acted as best man. It had all happened so suddenly that everyone present had trouble believing it was happening when the couple finally exchanged "I do's."

The two lovers had obtained a license the previous day in Riverside, California, in an effort to keep the event as secret as possible. But the press learned about Brando's marriage soon enough, and they immediately began to investigate the bride's background. There was something mysterious about Anna Kashfi; certain facts didn't check out. For example, she had given her parents' names as Devi and Selma Kashfi of Calcutta, India, when she and Brando had applied for their marriage license. But a quick check with contacts in India failed to uncover the Kashfis' whereabouts. Anna explained that her father had died several weeks earlier. Her mother, she said, had left Calcutta.

The press still was not satisfied. They contacted Dmytryk, who had brought Anna to America. Dmytryk said that he had met Anna in Paris when he was casting for *The Mountain*. He suggested that *Kashfi* might be a stage name and said that he assumed that Anna was Anglo-Indian.

Finally, the subject exploded. An Irish factory worker and his wife, who made their home in Cardiff, Wales, identified Brando's bride as their daughter, Joan. Mr. and Mrs. William Patrick O'Callahan told interviewers that they were happy about their daughter's marriage but couldn't quite understand her reluctance to reveal her true identity. According to the O'Callahans, Anna had indeed been born in Darjeeling, India, on September 30, 1934. Mr. O'Callahan had been working for the Indian rail system at the time. The alleged parents vigorously denied that Anna had so much as a drop of Indian blood in her veins.

Kashfi herself refuted the O'Callahans' story, maintaining that she had never even heard of the Irish couple who claimed her as their child, and even though Dmytryk later admitted that he had known all along that Anna's true family name was O'Callahan, she steadfastly refused to retract her original story.

Whether Brando knew Anna's true history is open to question. In view of his opinions on people's national origins, he probably didn't care much about his bride's. However, Brando's sister Frannie did tell newswriters that she was certain that her new sister-in-law was Indian, regardless of disclosures in the papers.

Although people in the United States and the rest of the world were confused about Anna's background, there was no doubt in the minds of the citizens of Cardiff, Wales, that one of their hometown girls had made good. Women who claimed to have been girlhood friends of Anna told the eager press about their early relationships with the shy Catholic girl; the O'Callahans' sons confirmed their parents' story; and an enterprising butcher in the Welsh town where Anna supposedly had been a clerk hung a sign in his window that read "Marlon Brando's Wife Once Worked Here."

While the debates about Anna's origins raged, the relationship between the newlyweds cooled.

They had rented a small house of exquisite Japanese design on Mulholland Drive in Coldwater Canyon, where such stars as James Cagney also had homes. Located on five acres of rugged terrain in the swank suburb, the house provided the Brandos with the privacy they wanted—in return for the $1,000-a-month rent. To make sure they weren't disturbed, the owner posted a sign on the property that read, "Unless you have an appointment, under no circumstances disturb the occupant."

However, Brando was rarely seen at home once he and his wife moved in. Almost immediately, he left for a few weeks. Following his return, he and Anna were seen occasionally at Hollywood parties, where they appeared to be happy. It was a good act. Close friends knew that Brando was only a part-time resident in his new home. He reportedly spent many nights at the apartment of his friend Sam Gilman.

Consequently, those who were close to the Brandos were hardly surprised when *Variety* announced in

December, 1957, that the marriage was on the rocks and that the couple would be separating. Brando made no comment. Anna, on the other hand, told reporters, "I could never depend on him. I had to spend too much of my life alone. My decision is final and conclusive—I was stupid to have gone through with it in the first place." She also announced that she was expecting a child. Hollywood columnists offered a variety of reasons for the breakup. Some said that Brando found his wife to be his intellectual inferior, that he soon ran out of things to talk to her about. Others said that Anna couldn't put up with Brando's offbeat lifestyle, which included frequent jaunts to such beatnik hangouts as the Co-Existence Bagel Shop in San Francisco.

Certainly the wealthy star was by no means a beatnik himself. Though he may have approved of some of the values of the rebellious movement (had, in fact, supplied them with a model through his own earlier behavior), he was not considered one of those described by Beat spokesman Jack Kerouac in his best-selling *On the Road:* "The ones who are mad to live, mad to talk, mad to be saved . . . the ones who never yawn or say a commonplace thing, but burn, burn, burn." However, the owner of one beat gathering place in San Francisco was ready to accept Brando, who stopped in occasionally, as a full-fledged Beat: "He's with us . . . he fights our fight in the middle of all that Hollywood junk."

The reporters and columnists soon grew uninterested in the alienated Brandos. After their initial statements, both refused to comment further. Then on May 11, 1958—seven months after the marriage—a son was born to the estranged couple. The reason for the marriage finally became clear and was confirmed later when Brando was quoted as saying cryptically that he got married in order to get divorced.

With her typical flair for the unusual, Anna named her son Christian Devi Brando. The choice was interesting on several counts. At the time of the marriage, Brando had just finished a picture in which his name had been Christian. As we have seen, Anna maintained that her "real" Indian father's name was Devi, and the name was of Indian origin (this was true, though the word means "goddess" in that language). At any rate, her selection reinforced what many of her former acquaintances had said about her. Anna presumably led a very rich fantasy life.

At first there was no talk of divorce. Then, in September, 1958, after a tragic accident in which Anna's maid was found drowned in the swimming pool of the Coldwater Canyon home, Anna and her son moved in with Pier Angeli (then separated from Vic Damone). A month later, Anna filed for divorce, charging "grievous mental suffering, distress, and injury." She flew to Hawaii with Christian; upon her return, she set up house in Beverly Hills. The divorce was granted in April, 1959. Anna received an initial cash settlement of $60,000 plus a $500,000 property settlement. The marriage was over, but the divorce was just the beginning of troubles that were to develop between Christian Brando's parents over his custody.

Anna, meanwhile, took a few courses at UCLA and made *Night of the Quarter Moon* in 1959 with Julie London and John Barrymore, Jr. It was to be her last picture until 1964, when she made an unsuccessful comeback with Rock Hudson in *Battle Hymn.*

Immediately following the separation in 1957, Brando was quite busy himself. He was working up a script for a Pennebaker movie in which he planned to star, and he was also on the lookout for other material that the new company might produce.

A previous Pennebaker venture was *Shake Hands with the Devil,* an adventure yarn about the Irish Revolution. Brando had considered playing the role of the young American who is recruited to the Irish cause when visiting that country. Other commitments, however, made his participation impossible, and young Don Murray, who was married to Hope Lange at the time, took over the role. It was an ambitious project, with a cast that included James Cagney, Michael Redgrave, Sybil Thorndike, and Glynis Johns. The film opened to favorable reviews but went nowhere—possibly due to distribution problems with United Artists.

Besides worrying over scripts for his own production company, Brando was also concerned about an outside script. Tennessee Williams had written a play called *Orpheus Descending,* and he had asked Brando to star in the 1957 Broadway opening. At the time the actor didn't care for the character he was to portray. Williams, a Brando admirer since *Streetcar* days, wanted the star so badly that he revised the role several times in an attempt to win him over. But Brando was not satisfied with any of the revisions, and even though Anna Magnani was to co-star, he refused the role. When *Orpheus Descending* flopped on Broadway, Williams was so angry with the way his play was cut up by the critics and ignored by the public that he vowed never again to mount one of his works on Broadway.

Still, there was talk of turning the stage failure into a movie. Again Brando was presented with script after script in an effort by Williams to persuade him to take the role of Val Xavier, the guitar-slinging wanderer in the snakeskin jacket.

Finally, Brando agreed to star in *The Fugitive Kind*— the new title given to Williams's work. He seemed to have a peculiar feeling about the film. But Anna Magnani and

Joanne Woodward were willing to take a risk. And Sidney Lumet, fresh from his success with *Twelve Angry Men,* was to direct, at the suggestion of Magnani.

Before shooting began, Brando decided to take a short vacation in Haiti with France Nuyen, then the Broadway star of *The World of Susie Wong.* Like Anna and other women to whom Brando had been attracted, the Franco-Chinese actress seemed to project a mysterious, exotic charm. The usual rumors sprouted about their relationship, and the press investigated with persistence. When Brando and Nuyen arrived in Miami after their two-week vacation, they were surrounded by reporters. Brando stalked past them without a word, and Nuyen tried to beat them off with her purse. Perhaps the short idyl had been long enough for each of them to realize that nothing more permanent could develop. They saw each other less in the months that followed, and rumors of a romance finally quieted down.

In July, 1958, filming of *The Fugitive Kind* began in Milton, New York—a small town located eighty miles north of Manhattan. As the crews set up their cameras, interested townspeople began lining the streets, most of them women hoping to catch a glance of Brando.

Their idol, meanwhile, was holed up in the local post office, which had been redesigned to look like a Southern general store. Brando was waiting for the technical crew to finish covering the streets of the small town with dirt in an effort to enhance the film's realism. Meanwhile, it looked as though it were going to rain cats and dogs.

Finally, Magnani and Woodward appeared, and Brando went out to meet them. The local women waved and shouted greetings to the star.

"Can I get you some nice homemade stew, Marlon?" one matron called out.

"No thanks, honey," he replied, "they're bringing me something."

Laughter and giggles poured from the sidelines. Brando, Magnani, Woodward, and Lumet huddled around the camera crew. Then, as Brando had feared, the rain came down in torrents. A bad omen? Lumet brushed it aside. He told his cast that they would shoot a scene from the middle of the movie that called for rain.

"Actually, it's a piece of luck," the director tried to cheer up his stars.

Nobody looked too happy or relieved. Brando drew aside to wait for his entrance and was cornered by the local newspaper reporter. The newsman glanced at the many women who were standing in the rain, waiting to get a look at Brando in action.

"What do you think of all our fine ladies ogling your way?" he asked.

"I don't know what to think. I'm just looking."

The critics confirmed Brando's fears about the film when it opened almost a year later. It cost almost $2 million to produce. It featured a cast of top talent and was the brainchild of America's most successful and esteemed playwright. But according to most observers, it was a failure.

McCarten advised his *New Yorker* readers that *The Fugitive Kind* was "cornpone melodrama." Stanley Kauffmann wrote in the *New Republic* that the work showed a bankruptcy of material on the part of Williams. Alpert said that the film gave him "the miseries" because of its "windy writing" and "dreary symbolism."

Almost alone among the major critics, Crowther found the effort worthwhile. Calling it a "piercing account of loneliness and disappointment in a crass and tyrannical world," he praised Brando and Magnani for their brilliant acting. He also applauded Lumet for his "perceptive understanding" and "outright audacity in pacing his film at a morbid tempo that lets time drag and passions slowly shape."

The public sided with the majority of the critics and stayed away in droves. To add insult to injury, Tennessee Williams was actually booed by movie patrons following a "sneak preview" at the RKO Theater on Fifty-Eighth Street in New York. Evidently, the audience was expecting *The FBI Story* and were a bit non-plussed at being subjected to the playwright's poetic mood piece. As he hurried outside, someone recognized him and shouted out, "There's Tennessee Williams, the guy who wrote that piece of junk we just saw." The crowd started to boo and hiss at him.

"I just booed back," Williams told the press.

About the kindest thing one can say about the film is that it was one of the first to explore the "outsider-*vs.*-the-redneck" theme that culminated in such later films as *Easy Rider*. *The Fugitive Kind* has some brilliant scenes between Brando and Magnani and also features some exquisite close-ups.

After the completion of *The Fugitive Kind,* Brando was offered the lead in *Lawrence of Arabia.* Friend Sam Spiegel was producing the epic and had already signed David Lean as director. But the portrait of the mysterious, egocentric Englishman apparently didn't appeal to Brando, and Peter O'Toole was eventually given the part.

Brando was still tied up with the second film he was planning for Pennebaker. He had yet to settle on a script and director, and he was beginning to have qualms about the amount of time and money he'd already spent on the project.

Too, Brando's critics were becoming increasingly vocal, asking when, if ever, he was going to live up to the promise of his early career. At the time, he must have felt that he was inhibited from realizing his full potential by the dearth of quality material, tight-fisted studio executives, and the inability of directors to understand his artistic objectives. Now, one obvious way to get around these obstacles would be to produce *and* direct his next film. And that is exactly what Brando did the next time he faced a camera.

8.

Actor as *Auteur*

CURRENTLY, the concept of the filmmaker as *auteur*—a person responsible for direction and production as well as for the script—is a popular subject of discussion among serious film critics. Griffith, Chaplin, Mankiewicz, Truffaut, and Fellini are among the most notable exponents of this unique approach to the art of the cinema. In most cases such filmmakers have graduated to the role of *auteur* from directorial ranks, though a few, such as Chaplin, Cassavetes, and Peter Fonda, began as actors.

Perhaps few commentators would consider Marlon Brando an *auteur* in the full sense of the word. But the idea may not be too farfetched.

Brando's concerns with the productions in which he's been involved have generally been broader than those of the typical actor. As we have seen, as early in his career as the Broadway version of *Streetcar,* he toyed with

Williams's lines, overstepped the limits of Kazan's direction, and experimented in other ways. His meticulous care for developing the character of Terry Malloy in *Waterfront* and his concern for establishing telling relationships with the other characters contributed as much toward the success of the film as did the direction of Kazan. Indeed, it was Brando who insisted on retakes of the famous cab scene with Rod Steiger, and it was Brando who worked Eva Marie Saint into a frenzy in an effort to achieve artistic integrity. And in later films, such as *Sayonara* and *Lions,* it was the actor as *auteur* who fought for crucial changes in scripts and direction that altered the whole meaning and impact of those works.

As far back as 1957 Brando had been thinking about making a movie through Pennebaker Productions—a project that would finally afford him the opportunity to test his own ideas on what cinematic art was all about. As can be seen in his interview with Capote, Brando wanted total control over such an effort—from the script (which he said he was helping to adapt from a novel) through production and direction.

The film that Brando was working on at that time was to be called *A Burst of Vermillion.* A western with plenty of shoot-'em-up action, it also carried a strong message about racial tolerance. Brando wanted his product to be both meaningful and entertaining—as well as financially successful.

Most critics feel that *A Burst of Vermillion* evolved into Brando's next picture, *One Eyed Jacks.* But if we compare the story line of *One Eyed Jacks* with that of the abandoned project, we can see that most probably they are two distinctly different films. *Vermillion* was to be organized around a theme of racial injustice; *Jacks* clearly uses the revenge motif as its jumping-off point.

There is other evidence to suggest that the two projects were distinct. Those who were involved in the initial stages of *One Eyed Jacks* trace the film's origin to a meeting between Frank P. Rosenberg, a Hollywood producer, and Charles Neider, who had just written a book titled *The Authentic Death of Henry Jones.* According to Rosenberg, the meeting took place in a Los Angeles Chinese restaurant in 1957. Rosenberg bought the idea of turning the book into a novel and agreed with Neider that Brando would be ideal for the lead. As they separated, the director told the author to work up a script. But Rosenberg warned Neider not to be too optimistic about obtaining Brando for their leading man. At the time, Brando was swamped with offers, and it was well known that he generally took years to respond—even negatively—to any offer.

Neider finished the script in April, 1958, almost a year after Brando had discussed *Vermillion* with Capote. The first version of *One Eyed Jacks* was sent to Brando by Rosenberg one Thursday afternoon. To Rosenberg's amazement, Brando called him the following day to express great interest in the story. By Saturday all arrangements except financing had been finalized between the two.

Subsequent progress was not so speedy, Rosenberg wanted rewrites of certain sections of the script. Brando agreed; he told Rosenberg that he thought the revisions could be completed in four weeks. Eight months later the script still was not satisfactory; Calder Willingham, novelist and screenwriter, was called in to assist.

Meanwhile, in August, 1958, Rosenberg went to Mexico City to find a Mexican leading lady for the film. After surveying a huge crop of unknowns, he narrowed his choice down to ten starlets. Rosenberg's final selection was Pina Pellicer, a shy girl with scant knowledge of the English language and negligible acting experience. She was brought to Hollywood and introduced to Brando, who approved of the choice.

Though the problem of a leading lady had been solved, troubles over the script continued to plague the production. When Willingham was unable to solve them, another writer, Guy Trosper, was called in. Discussions about the proposed picture took place from time to time in Brando's Coldwater Canyon home. In general the exchanges were friendly. When they became too heated, Brando would strike a huge brass gong in the teak-floored living room to restore order.

Finally, the group thought they had a script. But by this time Brando was tied up with *The Fugitive Kind.* When that film was completed, work on *Jacks* resumed. The new problem was to find a director.

Rosenberg suggested a few possibilities, and then Brando came up with the name of Stanley Kubrick. The star had been impressed with the former journalist's first two films, *The Killing* and *Paths of Glory.* Within a few weeks the young director was sitting in on the bull sessions for *One Eyed Jacks.*

The association proved to be short lived. Kubrick, who had both written and directed his first films and was a bit of an *auteur* himself, quickly saw that he and Brando would be at loggerheads about the final decisions that would have to be made on the film. He quickly withdrew from the project.

Consequently, by September, 1959, when filming was scheduled to begin, *Jacks* was still without a director. The cast—which included Karl Malden, Katy Jurado, Ben Johnson, Slim Pickens, and Brando's buddy, Sam Gilman—was already on the payroll. Who was going to put the whole thing together?

With mixed feelings, Brando suggested that he, himself, might direct. Rosenberg was not enthusiastic and felt that the film's other backers would be even less interested. The star had no directing experience; filming would be expensive (*Jacks* was to be shot in color): and Brando would also be playing the lead. On the other hand, payroll expenses were mounting, and the investors were beginning to scream for some kind of action. So in the end, Rosenberg relented.

At long last, in December, 1959, shooting began. The first day on the set—a Paramount lot in Monterey, California—Brando announced that he and the cast would improvise at first until they found a sense of direction. The announcement reportedly drove Rosenberg to a state of near nervous collapse. Any hopes of finishing the picture in the scheduled sixty days must have vanished from his mind.

Rosenberg must have grown even more despairing as he watched the new director at work. Brando examined every camera setup to make sure that he was getting the utmost from each shot. On one occasion he reportedly waited hours for the wind to whip up waves on the calm Pacific so that he could get the effect he wanted for the background. Rosenberg later revealed, "Every line every actor read, every button on every costume got his [Brando's] concentrated attention until he was completely satisfied."

Brando was as hard on himself as he was on the cast and crew. To achieve the effect that he wanted in a drunk scene, he guzzled a pint of vodka. He lost his lunch, but the vodka had served him well, and he printed the scene. On another occasion he dislocated his shoulder showing Karl Malden how to strike him with a large bullwhip. He hired a stuntman to play rehearsals of the scenes in which he was to appear, then quickly jumped into place as the cameras started rolling.

One Eyed Jacks was not finished until June, 1959. It had taken six months to complete instead of sixty days, but still Brando wasn't satisfied with the final product. He had been talked into changing the ending so that Pellicer wasn't killed, but the conclusion bothered him. He offered the matter up to the cast for a vote, which failed to decide anything. Finally, he determined to let the question jell in his mind, advising Rosenberg that another ending could be added later if necessary.

Rosenberg, meanwhile, was the object of screams of indignation and not-so-vague threats resulting from the costs of the production. Originally budgeted at $2 million, the film's final expenses came close to the $6 million mark.

When Rosenberg complained to his director, Brando said that he was shooting a movie, not a schedule.

Brando had shot almost a million feet of costly Technicolor film. To keep costs down, Brando agreed to print only 250,000 feet (still almost twice the length of an average picture). When Rosenberg sat down to view the unedited version, it was an incredible four hours and forty-two minutes. Obviously, some drastic cutting was needed.

With Rosenberg, Brando supervised the editing. The director agreed to drop an ancillary love story between the main character and a Chinese girl. Reacting as though his own flesh were being sliced away, Brando watched as foot after foot of beautiful, panoramic views and explosive acting were excised from the film. Finally, the picture was trimmed down to two hours and twenty-two minutes.

Brando still was not satisfied with the film's conclusion, however. Exercising certain rights that he had in the picture, he went out in October, three months after the film was reportedly finished, to shoot a new ending.

When the production finally was complete, the publicity campaign began. Brando didn't help matters much by relating his true feelings about the film to the press— often in the presence of his nervous public relations man. When asked if he liked directing, Brando responded, "It's like being an emotional traffic cop." He refused to say whether he'd attempt to direct again.

On another occasion Brando told a reporter, *"One Eyed Jacks* is just a product—like a news item. News makes money, not art. Movies aren't art."

And with bitter irony he said of the film, "It's not an artistic success. I'm a businessman. I'm a captain of industry—nothing less. Any pretensions I've sometimes had of being artistic are now a chilly hope."

It was not until March, 1961, that the picture finally opened in New York. Despite the negative comments of the film's director-star, the premier was given some encouraging advance publicity. *Life* again gave Brando a cover and devoted a photo-essay to the making of the picture. The movie magazines reported that fans were dying to see the results of $6 million and four years of their idol's time.

The majority of reviews were positive. Kauffmann in the *New Republic* hailed *One Eyed Jacks* as the vehicle for an important new directorial talent. Calling the film a kind of classic, Kauffmann noted its unusual length but added that it was never boring. On the other hand, Robert Hatch, a Brando aficionado, had few nice things to say. "It runs downhill for more than two hours," he wrote. Predictably, *Time* carped, "In short he plays the same character he's always played, the only character that really interests him: Marlon Brando. A childish thing indeed." But even *Time's* reviewer had to admit,

"It is meticulously produced and startlingly beautiful."

Alpert agreed with the "fierce, moody, flamboyant" star. *One Eyed Jacks,* he maintained, was a "slick, professional western," adding, "It is among the best of its type." McCarten found the direction confusing and the acting superb. "Brando is hypnotic," he wrote about a scene in which the star sits on a riverbank following a beating. "He sits shaken and drained, in an agony both physical and psychological that is absolutely private. The effect is devastating and, I should think, indelible."

Crowther was bothered by what he felt to be a mixture of contrasting styles. "It's as if it had been directed jointly by John Huston and Raoul Walsh," he quipped. On the one hand, he applauded the "vicious style that Mr. Brando has put into so many of his scabrous roles." On the other hand, he damned the lush scenic photography as something more appropriate to a travelogue on Hawaii.

Adding to Brando's professional difficulties at the time of the production of *Jacks,* were problems of a more personal nature. Almost as soon as Anna received her divorce, she began to cause trouble for her former husband over visitation rights with Christian. The court battles that ensued provided choice morsels for the gossip columnists. On one occasion, it was reported that Anna had broken into Brando's apartment and attacked him physically while he was entertaining a female visitor. On another, she was said to have threatened Brando with a knife when he came to pick up his son for a day's outing.

But what really made headlines in the spring of 1962, as the two embittered parents squared off in court again over custody of their three-year-old son, was the revelation that Brando had been secretly married in June of the previous year and had fathered another child.

Brando's second wife was his old friend from *Zapata* days, Movita. Details of the marriage are scarce, but most commentators assume that it took place in Mexico, where Brando and Movita resumed their relationship during the filming of *Jacks.* At the time of the disclosure, Movita was reported to be living in Hollywood with Brando and their infant son, Michael (referred to affectionately as Miko by his parents).

Anna was particularly disturbed by the fact that Brando had begun to take Christian to the home he shared with Movita so that his two sons could get to know each other. She attempted to disprove the legitimacy of Brando's second son, simultaneously challenging Brando's right to see Christian on the grounds that the star was morally unfit.

The imbroglio proved to be too much for Movita. Declaring that Hollywood was no fit place to raise children, she returned to Mexico in April, 1962. Still, Movita and Brando remained friendly, seeing each other over the years whenever the actor made his frequent visits to Miko.

A cloud of mystery hangs over Brando's second go at matrimony. In 1968, when his marriage to Movita was finally annulled in Santa Monica, California, it was revealed that the couple had had a second child, Rebecca, then two years old. No public record exists of the court hearings, so it is difficult to understand just how judge Harry Brand found it within his power to grant an annulment after the marriage had produced two children. Neither Movita nor Brando has ever felt compelled to comment on the matter. Content to remain on friendly terms, they have scrupulously avoided any publicity that might harm their two children.

The sailing of the H. M. S. *Bounty* from Lunenburg,

Nova Scotia, on October 10, 1960, was to set in motion another chain of events that would bring unwanted notoriety to Brando. Again, a dark, exotic woman was to be involved.

The ship, on its way on a projected 37-day voyage to Tahiti, was a replica (with certain modern engineering improvements) of the famous vessel that Captain Bligh had commanded when the mutiny immortalized by Nordhoff and Hall had set him adrift in the South Pacific during the late eighteenth century. It had been built at an estimated cost of $750,000 from plans of the original *Bounty* supplied by the British Naval Museum. The ship was on its way to Tahiti, where MGM would film its second version of *Mutiny on the Bounty*. The building and sailing of the ship plus the on-location shooting of the film were indications that MGM was sparing no expense in its attempt to surpass the original adaptation by Irving Thalberg. The 1935 version of *Mutiny on the Bounty,* starring Clark Gable and Charles Laughton, was already legendary.

Just how much MGM was willing to spend in its desperate move to produce a box-office smash that would bring a television-oriented public back to the movie houses was open to question. Supposedly, the film was originally budgeted at about $10 million, though insiders realized that it could easily exceed even that seemingly astronomical amount. As it turned out, the final cost was more than double the initial estimates, and the film nearly caused the downfall of the prestigious studio.

According to the predominantly hostile press, the near demise of MGM was due almost solely to the shenanigans and machinations of the picture's star—Marlon Brando. And when it became apparent that, despite its popularity at the box office, the film could never re-

coup the astounding production expenses, many felt
that Brando was singularly responsible for the death of
the Hollywood superstar system and the end of an era.
Movie companies, shocked by the example of Brando's
earnings on the film (and the salaries of such stars as
Elizabeth Taylor), began exploring other avenues than
superstars and extravaganzas to bolster their sagging
profits.

Within this context it is interesting to trace Brando's
involvement with the picture; for, though he apparently
capitalized on the misfortunes that plagued the production for three years, he was as much a victim of the
mismanagement of the filming as the studio itself.

Brando was first approached about the project sometime in late 1960 by producer Aaron Rosenberg. The
role of Fletcher Christian, immortalized by Gable, was
choice. But Brando seemed unenthusiastic about a section of the script written by veteran Eric Ambler, and so
he declined Rosenberg's offer.

Shortly afterward, Brando reread the Nordhoff and
Hall book for the first time since his youth. He felt that
both the 1935 film and the Ambler section of the adaptation missed the main point of the story. In his opinion
the significance of the book was not in the details surrounding the mutiny itself but in the fact that even after
the mutineers had freed themselves of Bligh, they failed
to build a worthwhile society or find any happiness. It
was clear to Brando that the picture should concentrate
on the fate of the mutineers once they established themselves on Pitcairn Island.

He later told a critic, "Here was a group of men who
conquered tyranny in the mutiny. They had a great
opportunity to achieve happiness. But what happened?
Within two years most of them were dead—from having
killed one another."

Brando called Rosenberg and outlined his ideas; the producer was interested. After preliminary negotiations, it was agreed that Brando would receive a $500,000 guaranteed advance against 10 percent of the receipts plus certain consultation rights on the script. In addition, sensing Rosenberg's and the studio's confusion about the film and suspecting that the studio might attempt to tie him up time-wise if he insisted on having his say about the script, Brando demanded and won a provision that awarded him a daily salary of $5,000 should the shooting go beyond the original schedule. This shrewd move reportedly provided him with overtime pay of $1.25 million by the time the picture was finally in the can.

Once the contract had been worked out, Carol Reed, the film's English director, was flown to Hollywood to meet his star. Evidently, the meeting was not too productive of good will. Reed later reported that Brando spent most of their first discussion attempting to persuade the director to make a film about convicted California rapist Caryl Chessman, who was soon to be executed. Reed was noticeably cool on Brando's ideas about *Mutiny on the Bounty*. About the only concrete result of the meeting was a decision to select a native girl to play the role of Brando's South Sea sweetheart.

To help select the young woman, Brando went to the island paradise sometime around the end of 1960. One local beauty after another was brought to his hotel room for an interview. Among the tricks Brando used to test the girl's potential was to threaten to throw himself out of his second-story window. Most of the girls failed the crude screen test, unable to come up with anything more dramatic than frightened giggles.

Finally, however, Brando was struck by the beauty and sensitivity of one young girl. Her name was Tarita, and she worked in a small local hotel. She registered real fear and emotion as Brando perched on his window ledge: he knew that he had found his leading lady.

The first delay in filming resulted from a stupid oversight. Neither Reed, his production staff, nor any of the studio heads had taken into account the rainy season, which inundated the island every year as regularly as clockwork. The crews and the actors had to pack their bags and return to Hollywood.

Other difficulties combined with the forces of nature to keep the *Bounty* off course. There was also the matter of directors and a final script. After final editing, Reed's total contribution to the finished product amounted to about five minutes of film. Louis Milestone, an old pro whose credits included *The Front Page, Of Mice and Men,* and *A Walk in the Sun,* subsequently took Reed's place at the helm in an attempt to salvage the floundering vessel.

After it was all over, Milestone said, "I've been in the business a few days, but I never saw anything like this. It was like a ship without a rudder in a hurricane without a captain. I thought when I took the job it would be a nice trip. By the time I was finished, I felt like I'd been shanghaied."

More significant are Milestone's comments on Brando's role in the *Bounty* fiasco: "The big trouble was lack of guts at Metro. Lack of vision when they saw the kind of trouble they were into. They should have stopped the whole damned production. And if they didn't like Marlon's behavior, they should have told him to do as they wished or taken him out of the picture.

"Marlon didn't have approval of the story," he continued, "but he did have control over himself. If Brando didn't like something, he would just stand in front of the camera and not act. At the same time he was right in many of the things he wanted."

Then there were the writers and their various scripts.

The first version was a combination of the work of three men. Eric Ambler wrote the first third of the story (up to the mutineers' arrival on Tahiti), William L. Driscoll handled the second third (life on Tahiti), and Borden Chase worked on the remainder (the mutineers' lives on Pitcairn Island). The studio somehow expected the three sections to fit together as neatly as the parts of a jigsaw puzzle.

The results of the collaboration were highly unsatisfactory, and MGM hired Charles Lederer to make some sense of the mess. It turned out to be more than just a paste-and-patch job; almost a complete rewrite was needed.

While Lederer was busy chopping out the copy, shooting began—slowly. Since Brando had definite ideas as to what the film was ultimately to be about, and since his contract gave him a degree of control over the script, he was unwilling to settle for hastily made compromises or ill-considered decisions.

Almost from the start, the studio heads were no longer interested in preserving any degree of artistic integrity. They wanted the picture finished so that it could earn back some of the money they'd already spent on the project. Brando, by contrast, knew what he wanted and decided to play a waiting game till the moguls came around to his way of thinking.

Before long, the rumors started flying: it was Brando that had "gone native," that he refused to work, that he spent all his time eating, dancing, swimming, and otherwise funning with the ebullient Tahitians. And, of course, there was talk of a new romance—this time with his eighteen-year-old leading lady, Tarita.

Brando's relationship with Tarita ultimately produced two children—a son, Tehotu, born sometime around 1963, and a daughter, Tarita Cheyenne, born in 1970. In the Tahitian culture a couple become married when they set up housekeeping together. Consequently, as Tarita explained to a magazine reporter years later, she and Brando saw no need for a formal marriage ceremony.

As the weeks of delay turned into months, Brando worked at developing his part. He certainly didn't want to mimic Gable's portrayal of Fletcher Christian. Milestone agreed with Brando and told a reporter, "He's too cerebral to play the part the way Gable did." As for his own interpretation, Brando commented later: "My part is that of a man who is intuitive and suspicious, proud, and searching. He has a touch of the vain and a childish and disproportionate sense of virtue and manly ethics. He is lonely and generally distrustful of human contacts."

Brando had persuaded his boyhood friend, Bob Hoskins, to leave his Libertyville home and become a dialogue director on location in Tahiti. Hoskins later described one device that the star used to develop Fletcher Christian's rather affected manner of speaking. Brando would go around for days on end reciting from a book of English lyric poetry in a Yorkshire accent. Within a few weeks he had what he wanted and could concentrate on developing the finer points in his portrayal.

In May, 1961, the studio announced—prematurely—that, except for a few final scenes, the picture was complete. All that was needed was a script for the end of the film, which would be shot when Brando, who had begun work on another picture, again became available. Lederer again got busy, then had to withdraw temporarily due to personal troubles while old pro Ben Hecht filled in for him. Finally, Lederer returned to assist Hecht, and the two writers felt they had something that everyone would buy. Unfortunately, Marlon Brando didn't buy.

But in late spring of the following year the reluctant

star evidently had a change of heart. He went to Rosenberg and asked to see the film, which he pronounced "pretty damn good." Brando made a few suggestions about the script; they were quickly approved; and the star suggested that the company take two weeks to bring the listing *Bounty* into port. As a token of his sincerity, Brando agreed to work for two weeks with no salary while they wrapped it up.

By this time, Milestone realized that *Mutiny on the Bounty* was really as much Brando's picture as it was his. So for the final scenes, Milestone stayed in the background while Brando acted as director. There seemed little point at that late date in discouraging Brando from playing *auteur*.

Finally, with great fanfare the studio announced in June, 1962, that *Mutiny on the Bounty* was really finished. One commentator noted that the film had taken three years to produce and had cost almost $25 million. Brando's weight had varied between 170 and 210 pounds during the course of shooting, and he was responsible for at least one pregnancy among the local girls. In addition, three members of the original cast had died during the filming period. Milestone pointed out that the total costs exceeded those of *Gone with the Wind* and *Ben Hur* combined.

It was not until November, 1963, that the anxiously awaited premier was held on a reserved-seat basis at Loew's State in New York and the Egyptian Theater in Los Angeles. The press went to work at once. Leading off was a cover story in the *Saturday Evening Post* titled "The Mutiny of Marlon Brando," which laid the blame for the astronomical cost of the film squarely on the star's shoulders. Allegedly quoting Milestone and cast members Trevor Howard and Richard Harris, the article implied that Brando had deliberately sabotaged the film.

Brando sued the magazine for $4 million, charging that the article contained false and libelous statements. But the damage had already been done.

Next to jump on the bandwagon was Dwight MacDonald. His article in *Esquire* attacked Brando on a personal basis and took the actor to task for attempting to project some meaning into his portrayal and the film.

The critics were only a trifle kinder. Gill of the *New Yorker* called Brando's Christian a "sea-going Hamlet." Kauffmann found the actor "hard to take seriously" because of the roles that Brando had played in the past. Arthur Knight in *Saturday Review* characterized Brando's performance as a "curious one." Crowther's review began, "You will have to wait a long time to beat what you will see in *Mutiny on the Bounty.*" The article proceeded to question the validity of the character Brando created and concluded by calling the picture "lumpish." And even Pauline Kael, writing later, found his efforts "like a Dead End Kid playing Congreve." She pronounced it a "joke."

If the critics had been more astute, they might have realized that Brando's Fletcher Christian was an outgrowth of a character type that he had been polishing and developing since he had appeared as Marchbanks opposite Katharine Cornell. Certainly, some aspects of this alter-ego to his rebel image can be seen in Brando's Napoleon, Sergius, Major Gruver, and the German officer in *Lions*. And seen in this light, Brando simply was bigger than his Hollywood stereotype.

Despite the fact that many members of the press and film industry blamed Brando for the failure of *Mutiny on the Bounty,* there were those who stuck up for him. Rosenberg, the producer, who certainly would have had every reason to finger Brando if he had been the real culprit, remarked, "He felt we weren't living up to the agreements we had made with him on the basic concepts of the picture. Besides, with an actor like Brando, he has to feel the part, so you have to allow him to make contributions to the script and directing. Otherwise, he can't work."

Even Anna came to Brando's defense, saying that he had been victimized by the press.

When Brando himself was asked to comment on the failures of such big-budget extravaganzas as *Bounty* and *Cleopatra,* he remarked, "The reason for all the recent big film failures is about the same. Briefly, it is the lack of a working script."

Such defenses and explanations didn't impress the Hollywood establishment. After the production costs were totaled for *Jacks* and *Bounty,* Brando was more out of favor than ever. He told one interviewer, "I feel I may be coming to the end of my acting career." Judging from the box office response to his two latest films, he probably was right.

After the failure of *Bounty,* the studios stopped pestering Brando for the really big pictures that were coming up. In a way, this seemed to suit him just fine. He was becoming quite a world traveler, bouncing around the globe to keep up with his interests, friends, and various families. And apparently he began to feel that if he couldn't be a force for social improvement as an *auteur,* he could still do some good as an actor. Better yet, he could provide an example through his personal life that just might wake up a few people. If Hollywood didn't care for his two-pronged attack, well, they knew what they could do about it.

9.

Rebel with a Cause

As was the case with other screen rebels of the late forties and fifties—Montgomery Clift, withdrawn and intellectual; James Dean, the crazy mixed-up kid; and Paul Newman, the roughneck heel—Brando seemed to be *against* a great many intangibles rather than *for* anything concrete.

After John F. Kennedy took office and the civil rights movement gained momentum, the mood of the country seemed to shift from complacency to activism. It became time for people of goodwill to speak out, and Brando was among the first of the Hollywood notables to do so.

Some years later, Brando was asked when he first became interested in the civil rights movement. He stated, "I guess it all really started for me when Mrs. Rosa Parks refused to sit in the back of the bus in Birmingham, Alabama." Once he made up his mind to support

151

the movement, his commitment was total and personal.

In March, 1961, Brando's name, along with those of Eleanor Roosevelt, Nat King Cole, Harry Belafonte, Sidney Poitier, and others appeared in an ad in the *New York Times* that solicited funds for Martin Luther King, Jr., and his Southern Christian Leadership Conference and was highly critical of the way demonstrators for black rights in Alabama were being treated by the police. The mayor of Montgomery was so incensed that he filed a $500,000 lawsuit against the paper.

Later, Brando showed up with Paul Newman, Tony Franciosa, and Virgil Frye in Gadsden, Alabama, in an attempt to establish a liaison between white city officials and black leaders involved in demonstrations. When Mayor Lesley Gilliand refused to see the actors, they tried to get into the executive offices of a nearby Republic Steel plant to discuss that company's discriminatory hiring policies. Again they failed, and the local papers accused them of being rabble-rousers.

Brando, serving as spokesperson for the group, told a crowd of reporters gathered for a press conference, "We are here as devoted and peaceful representatives of goodwill, not as agitators, interlopers, or interferers.

"While no one can deny that Negroes have not achieved racial equality in the South, we have trouble in New York, in the West, the East and the North. Southerners can point to the North and accuse them of hypocrisy, insulated and restrictive thinking, just as easily as the finger can be pointed the other way. Too long the South has been accused as the sole source of friction and trouble between the races. They are just as much to blame in the North, East and West."

On another occasion Brando joined Sammy Davis, Jr., and Burt Lancaster in Mississippi to gather support for a voter registration drive. Davis told reporters, "Marlon's a stand-up guy with the courage of his convictions. He and Burt and I came down here to show the Negroes that other Negroes and white people aren't afraid to give them moral support."

Brando's activities were not confined to the South. In keeping with his speech at Gadsden, he fought prejudice all over the country. In the West he led a march with Parnell Roberts (then appearing in TV's "Bonanza" series) to protest the discriminatory policies of a Torrance, California, all-white housing project. An angry crowd of the development's inhabitants booed and hissed the 125 marchers, and later 33 arrests were made. On the East Coast he was scheduled to appear at demonstrations in Maryland when he suffered an attack of pyelonephritis—a kidney disturbance—and had to cancel the engagements. Detractors accused him of copping out, and though his doctor confirmed the seriousness of the illness—at the same time revealing that Brando had four kidneys—Brando's critics would not be stilled.

But it wasn't long before the actor was back on his feet. In August, 1963, he joined such notables as James Baldwin, Charlton Heston, and Harry Belafonte at the base of the Lincoln Memorial during the first Washington march. Later, he appeared with Martin Luther King, Jr., at a fund-raising rally in Los Angeles. And after King's assassination, when the Poor People's March on Washington was being planned, Brando appeared at a special benefit at the Apollo Theater in Harlem. At the March itself, he and Joan Baez spoke to massive crowds.

People wondered what Brando was getting out of the civil rights movement. Many pointed out that his box-office appeal would certainly drop among certain groups.

"The Negro is benefiting me today," he told such inquirers, "because he is underscoring things that need underscoring. By taking his stand, he shows America's lack of commitment to such principles as freedom of speech and civil rights. Everyone should be enlisted in the movement for civil rights. It benefits all of us."

Brando practiced what he preached. When his personal secretary left him in 1964, he hired a black girl, Joy Anderson, to replace her. Earlier that same year, in an antiapartheid speech in London's Central Hall, he stated that for all his future contracts he would insist on a clause that would keep his films from being shown in segregated theaters. He contributed thousands to the cause of civil rights; at one rally alone he volunteered $5,000 and later increased the offer to a day's pay. Finally, some years later he began dating black singer Diana Ross.

Within the movie industry he urged the Screen Actors Guild to put pressure on the studios so that more black actors could obtain parts. He went out of his way to bring black actors to the attention of producers and studio casting directors. Seemingly, in his opinion the civil rights movement would be best served by pictures that showed whites and blacks working together without any consciousness of race.

Years later Brando attended the funeral of slain Black Panther Bobby Jones Hutton in Oakland, California. As reporters and photographers milled around, he told the mourning Panthers, "You've been listening 400 years to white people and they haven't done a thing. I'm going to begin right now informing white people what they don't know."

He made good on the promise a few weeks after the funeral. During a nationally televised appearance on the "Joey Bishop Show," he was highly critical of the killing of Hutton by the Oakland police. As a result, he was—unsuccessfully—sued for slander by that police agency.

Black Americans were not the only group Brando sought to help. In 1964 he met with some people from the National Congress of American Indians to discuss ways of making the nation aware of the Indians' plight. Brando offered financial aid and told the group about a documentary he was planning on the plight of the original Americans. (The projected picture has not yet been made, though Brando still is interested in the idea.)

In that same year he also attempted to meet secretly with the recently widowed Jacquelyn Kennedy to discuss a program of aid to mentally retarded children. Jacquelyn, her sister, Lee Radziwill, George Englund, and Brando hid behind dark glasses in an exclusive French restaurant in Washington, but the meeting broke up quickly when the group became the target for flashing cameras and questioning reporters.

All this activity on Brando's part did not escape the notice of certain departments of the government. As far back as 1958 Brando had complained to Truman Capote that he was under surveillance, that his personal life was being spied upon by some unknown government agency. Brando suspected that there was a tap on his telephone, and he told the skeptical writer (who treated the charge as if the actor were a bit paranoid) that when he and his friends spoke over the phone, they used a combination of hipster lingo and French to discuss their personal lives.

It did seem like an incredible charge. Why would anyone want to monitor a movie star's phone conversations or pry into his personal life? Yet Brando's charge was later reinforced when columnist Jack Anderson accused the FBI of snooping on such people as Brando, Harry Belafonte, Ralph Abernathy, Muhammad Ali, and Joe Namath. Reports of their activities allegedly made favorite bedtime reading for former president Lyndon Johnson.

Doubtless of even greater concern to such government snoopers was Brando's opposition to the U.S. involvement in Southeast Asia. After the star had met with President Sukarno on one of his visits to Indonesia, he became increasingly critical of the U.S. position. Around 1958, after reading *The Ugly American,* Brando became even more outspoken about what he seemed to feel was disastrous American foreign policy.

Director and friend George Englund evidently shared Brando's feelings. In addition, Englund thought that the book, which had sold nearly 400,000 hardcover copies and almost 2 million paperbacks by this time, would make a timely and important movie. Brando and Englund arranged a meeting with authors William J. Lederer and Eugene Burdick and subsequently bought the film rights for $100,000.

Work on *The Ugly American* couldn't begin immediately. Brando was tied up with *Mutiny on the Bounty* and either couldn't or wouldn't break away. Besides, a revamp of the book's story line would be necessary since the situation in Southeast Asia was changing so rapidly. Authors Lederer and Burdick later advised, "If the movie were to be just like the book, it would seem as dated as a Gibson Girl outfit."

Finally, screenwriter Stewart Stern, in cooperation with Brando, Englund, and the original authors, got busy on the script. The film was to be shot in Thailand, using native talent whenever possible. American cast members included Pat Hingle, Sandra Church, and another Brando: Jocelyn. Marlon's sister would play the wife of an American construction boss.

Production of *The Ugly American* was sandwiched between Brando's stints on *Mutiny*. Off and on during the almost two years it took to complete shooting *American,* Brando roamed around the countryside, meeting the people of Thailand, learning their customs. On one occasion, he stopped to talk to a withered old Thai woman standing beside the road. When she asked him what he did to earn his living, he thought for a moment and then laughingly said, "I make faces."

The U.S. government was very interested in what Brando and the rest of the film's company were doing. The story unfolded in a fictitious country named Sarkhan, but it was obvious that Sarkhan was just a pseudonym for Vietnam. The State Department offered to supply advisers, hoping that Brando's American ambassador wouldn't turn out too "ugly."

Such offers were politely refused. The film was shot under tight security conditions, and no one would comment on how the original novel had been changed or how Brando would play the part.

Wearing a neatly clipped moustache, an ambassadorial morning coat, and striped trousers, Brando obviously was attempting again a characterization that did not conform to his Hollywood stereotype. But there are certain resemblances between the urbane, self-satisfied Ambassador Harrison Carter MacWhite and Brando's Fletcher Christian.

The film premiered in America in April, 1963, and the critics' response is testimony to Brando's acting ability. Kauffmann in the *New Republic* maintained that the role of MacWhite was unlike anything the star had ever done before. Kauffmann liked what he saw but echoed Kael's opinion that the role just wasn't big enough for Brando's talent. Gill in the *New Yorker* offered "six cheers for Brando." He continued, "His portrayal is a pleasant surprise . . . he's as brilliant in this picture as he was dull in *Mutiny on the Bounty*. Gill opined that the character of MacWhite was a "Brando creation, purged completely of whomever Brando himself might be." Crowther called the star's performance "brilliant" and concluded: "Mr. Brando moves through the whole picture with authority and intelligence."

Even authors Lederer and Burdick were pleased with the final result—a situation all too rare when popular novels are adapted to the screen. They wrote, "As a work of art, the movie is more seamless, coherent, and compelling than our book."

Not the least of the picture's fans were the people of Thailand. During the course of his frequent forays into the Thai countryside, Brando had developed quite a following. It was a case of mutual admiration. In a short ceremony preceding the film's world premier in Bangkok, Brando told the audience, "There are too many ambassadors here. Every Thai is an ambassador. Since I have been here, I have never seen a face of despair. If every Thai could be sent out as a member of the Peace Corps, as an ambassador of love and goodwill, it would ease tensions."

Besides his work in pictures, his efforts on behalf of the civil rights movement, and his ongoing battle with Anna over seeing Christian, Brando was kept busy on a number of other fronts in 1963. In April he agreed to appear on David Susskind's television show, "Open End," in order to answer slurs and charges made in certain magazines and gossip columns.

Appearing with him were George Englund and author Eugene Burdick. Perhaps Susskind felt that it would be wise to include the actor's friends on the program to keep Brando in line. During a previous appearance on the "Wendy Barrie Show," Brando had reportedly feigned sleep when the questions became what he considered inane or too personal. When the interviewer managed to rouse him with a question about what his next picture would be, he yawned, "I forget."

Susskind began the program by asking Brando why he was so protective about the details of his personal life, why he was so hostile to the media. Brando maintained that most gossip columnists and reporters for movie magazines exploited their knowledge of actors' private lives. Brando continued, "I have two children [Christian and Miko] growing up in the community, and I think that both they and their mothers deserve protection."

In the following colloquy on the values of contemporary American society, Susskind seemed to slyly attack Brando for being more concerned with making money than with producing worthwhile movies. In reply, Brando asked Susskind how he rationalized working for a cigarette sponsor when it was known that cigarettes cause cancer.

Later that year, Brando's personal life again was invaded by the press when a young Filipino dancer named him in a paternity suit. "Brando Is the Father of My Child," screamed headlines in various movie publications. The dishonored mother, according to her story, had met Brando on his travels through the South Pacific. The relationship had allegedly grown serious, and when Brando returned to Hollywood, she maintained that she went with him.

Characteristically, Brando remained mute on the charges. He went into court and demanded a blood test. The test proved that he could not have been the father of the child; but again his name had been touched by scandal.

Meanwhile, he found time to become involved with two new productions. One of these was a "short" made for UNICEF, *Tiger by the Tail*, and it offered a timely message about tolerance.

The other, originally titled *King of the Mountain*, was another Pennebaker effort. After such weighty films as

Bounty and *The Ugly American,* Brando possibly felt
that a jaunt into the world of comedy might be nice for
a change. The star chose an original screenplay by Stanley Shapiro and Paul Henning. Ultimately, the title was
changed to *Bedtime Story.* Brando played a con artist
out to seduce maidens on the French Riviera. Ralph
Levy was lured from the medium of television to direct
the film; top stars David Niven and Shirley Jones were
recruited for other principal roles. Universal agreed to
handle distribution.

The shooting—partially on location in the south of
France—went off without a hitch. The only trouble oc-
curred when Brando suffered a mild flare-up of the kidney trouble that was beginning to plague him. When
Bedtime Story was finished, the company felt they had
a nice, tight commercial comedy.

The critics who bothered to review the film for the
most part agreed with the company. Kauffmann called
it a "screwball comedy" and praised Brando's mugging,
lunatic antics, and farcical style. Alpert found some of
the scenes howlingly funny but complained that the
overall effect was "sniggeringly dirty." In addition, he
wondered about a certain scene in which Brando appears in a wheelchair. He pointed out that there is a
similar scene in *The Men* and suspected that Brando was
parodying himself. Crowther was behind the picture 100
percent. "Marlon Brando is full of surprises," he wrote.
"That's part of his stock in trade. He loves to do the
unexpected and then sit back and let his public gasp.
That's what he's doing in *Bedtime Story* . . . . He is
departing from his usual style and playing a ring-a-ding
comedy character." The critic summed up: *"Bedtime
Story* is a very funny picture, and Mr. Brando is a first-
class farceur."

The public, however, didn't take the word of the

critics. Evidently they were unwilling to accept their rebel in a role that was more typical of Jack Lemmon or Cary Grant. In any case, the film was only a moderate box-office success, and commentators chalked up another Brando loser.

Perhaps in reaction, Brando next turned to melodramatic adventure. The following year, when Aaron Rosenberg told him about a spy yarn in which he could play an anti-Nazi German who aids the Allies in World War II, Brando said he was interested. The script had a message about involvement and was to feature such other stars as Trevor Howard and Yul Brynner.

It is interesting that Rosenberg sought Brando out after the alleged difficulties he had had with the star on *Mutiny*. Also noteworthy is the fact that Howard, who reportedly had said that he would never work with Brando again after *Mutiny,* was to be in the picture. Brando read the script, could find nothing wrong with it, and asked only a few favors: how about casting his old friends Wally Cox and William Redfield in the picture? There were a couple of roles that were just made for them.

Rosenberg agreed; the film was shot and in the can in record time. The only thing that bothered the director was the title—*Mori-Turi.* How would the public react to it? Would they realize that it was a spy story?

At the last minute, the title of the film was changed to *The Saboteur: Code Name—Mori-Turi.* It was a doubtful improvement; few movie marquees were able to accommodate the unwieldy title when the film moved from the first-run houses to the outlying theaters.

To pump up interest in the film, the backers placed Brando in New York's posh Hampshire House and fed him an endless stream of television interviewers. The tapings that followed were an amalgam of high jinks, put-ons, and soft sell. When Brando cut up with Bill Gordon of San Francisco's KGO-TV, the camera crew could barely keep from breaking up with laughter.

"I'll bet this new film of yours is really a great one—right Marlon?" asked Gordon.

"It sure is, pal," Brando replied, tongue in cheek. "Of course, all the pictures they make in Hollywood are really great films. Everybody knows that!"

"Right, Marlon. Why, they haven't made a bad picture in . . . "

"Ninety years!" the star interjected.

"I'm with you, Marlon."

"Well, it's really been great talking to you, Bill," Brando concluded. "Gee—that's some swell checkered coat you've got on there. And don't forget: vote for Wilkie!"

Neither the title change nor Brando's zany promotion helped the film. Except for Crowther, who felt that Brando's skillful and exciting performance didn't save a turgid story, the critics simply ignored *The Saboteur*. And the public, perhaps due to confusion over the title, or possibly because the film had distribution problems, never really seemed to be aware of Brando's latest offering.

Brando himself stayed in the public eye largely because of continuing troubles with Anna. In December, 1964, Christian, then six, called the police after finding his mother unconscious in their home. Anna maintained that she had passed out from the effect of pills she was taking to control epilepsy, an illness that supposedly had plagued her for five years. Brando obtained a court order giving him temporary custody of his son, and a hearing was set for early 1965. When a court officer attempted to serve Anna with a summons, she attacked him, thus alienating herself from the presiding judge. Finally, after a series of delays allegedly caused by Anna's poor health, the judge ordered a six-month cooling-off period, and Christian went to live with Brando's sister in Mundelein, Illinois.

Almost immediately, Anna began a slur campaign in the movie magazines against her former husband. In an exposé in *Photoplay* titled "Marlon Brando Is Out to Destroy Me—and He Will," she alleged that their marriage had failed because her husband didn't know what color their child would be when it was born. Supposedly, the champion of civil rights was a secret racist.

Brando made regular visits to his son until October, 1965, when Anna again went to court and obtained custody. Later, she was to maintain that Christian had been ruined by his enforced separation from her. Parents of children who attended the same summer camp as Christian don't corroborate Anna's charge. One woman remembers meeting Brando at one of the camp's Parents' Days. She had a pleasant chat with the proud father, who then introduced her to his son. The woman recalls that Christian seemed to be a happy, outgoing child who was enjoying his "vacation."

During this period Brando underwent two unfortunate experiences. The first was his fortieth birthday. Imagine—Marlon Brando was middle-aged! In a lengthy interview with Joanne Stang in the *New York Times,* he discussed the myths that had sprung up about his personality and private life. "It's all a fairy tale. But some people have a peculiar need to have fairy tales repeated to them. They like to imagine people in terms of certain identities, and they don't want them to play other roles in their fantasies. And, of course, much newswriting helps perpetuate fairy stories."

The inevitable questions regarding Brando's career

came up. How did he feel about acting; had he overcome his earlier ambivalent feelings about his
profession?

I've spent most of my career trying to figure out what I'd
really like to do. Of course, I have to make a living to support
my children and wives. But I have a variety of interests—reading, traveling, meeting people—which have been as important
to me as acting. Maybe more important. It may be hard to
believe, but acting has never been a dominant factor in my life.
I have no overwhelming interest in becoming a classical actor. I
don't think I would have stayed in theater if I hadn't gone to
Hollywood.

The second unfortunate event was the death of his
father, Marlon, Sr., at the age of seventy. Brando and his
father had grown increasingly close since Dodie's death.
Marlon, Sr., president of Pennebaker, had expertly guided his son's business interests in various areas so that
Brando could be free to follow other pursuits. Brando
often took his father along on filmmaking expeditions,
both to keep him up to date on business developments
and because they enjoyed each other's company.

At the time of his father's death, Brando was at work
on a new film—*The Chase.* Scripted by prestigious Lillian Hellman, who had taken more than a year to adapt
the novel and play by Horton Foote, the film was tout-
ed as a new kind of intelligent, adult Hollywood movie.
Producer Sam Spiegel, fresh from his success with *Lawrence of Arabia,* had obtained the services of Arthur
Penn as director. The forceful Penn, who had made his
name in television, had little respect for Hollywood and
had let it be known that his vision would guide any film
with which he became involved.

People wondered how Penn's position would sit with
Brando. Penn later commented, "We had a good ex-

change of ideas. Marlon told me at the outset that he would present me with ideas and that if I didn't like them I should let him know. That's the way it went. And, incidentally, most of his ideas were excellent."

The film was to be a testing ground for new talent. Robert Redford was assigned the role of the young fugitive; Jane Fonda was to be his slutty wife. Robert Duval and Jocelyn Brando were also featured. Such established stars as E. G. Marshall, Angie Dickinson, Janice Rule, and Martha Hyer provided balance.

The story, centering around the plight of a young escaped prisoner whom the sheriff of a small, Southern town tries to save from a modern lynch mob, was typical of a number of films of the day that strained to show the seamy side of American society. *The Chase* went slightly overboard in making its points. Though it strained to be realistic, some of the action was implausible, and several of the characters were little more than stereotypes.

Hellman, who had sweated over the script after a fifteen-year absence from Hollywood, was somewhat less than satisfied with the finished product. "The film marks the end of an old and foolish dream that I could write a picture just like I write anything else," she stated. "Decision by democratic majority is fine for government, but it's a stinky way to create." Hellman claimed that the studio's interference "slicked-up and mauled" her script. The women, she complained, all turned up "with three breasts."

The critics were not much kinder. The film was almost universally panned as a piece of propaganda; most reviewers found Penn's use of violence gratuitous and the characters wooden. Yet Brando garnered some favorable notices in the *Nation, Commonweal,* and *Newsweek.* Hatch wrote, "He is good, but then he is almost always good. You can't take your eyes from him.

He gets the results he needs with an economy of means that is theater poetry." Crowther, on the other hand, remained unimpressed: "The character assigned him is ambiguous and gross, and Mr. Brando cannot make it any more than a stubborn, growling cop."

At this point, Brando should have been pretty low. He was no longer young; the death of his father had meant the loss of a good friend and invaluable adviser; and it was obvious that his troubles with his first wife were far from over. Other problems included Brando's eroding box-office appeal, the antagonism of the studios, and the failure of Pennebaker to provide the money he needed to make the kinds of films he felt were important.

To make matters worse, after finishing *The Chase,* Brando became involved in a traditional horse opera, which bombed despite some good work on his part. Bearded and shaggy-haired for *The Appaloosa,* he played a foolhardy saddle bum who charges into enemy Mexican territory to rescue his stolen horse. Not many critics took notice of the film, and those who did found Brando's work a replay of the character he had created for *Jacks.*

Certainly, these developments could have led to a certain disillusionment on Brando's part. He confessed, "I don't think that under the present setup in Hollywood, you can really get a message across. And even if you do, I'm not sure how much good it would do."

Nonetheless, Brando's friends noted that he appeared happier, less uptight than he had been in his younger days. Seemingly gaining self-awareness and insight, he was evidently able to see the benefits that acting had provided him. "The opportunities offered an actor to pursue his curiosities are far greater than in most professions," he told an interviewer. "I would not have been able to meet President Sukarno, Professor Burdick, Dr. Hutchins or—what do you call it—The Fund for the Republic. I once gave a dinner for twenty people from the Rand Corporation. I couldn't have done that if I weren't an actor."

Brando continued to lend his personal and financial support to the civil rights and antiwar movements, among others. But at the same time he maintained a low profile to protect his personal life. There was a lot of living to be done. He had his children to keep up with, and if a good movie came his way occasionally, so much the better. His drive to do something worthwhile was probably still there, but Brando had shifted into a cruising gear that made his journey a bit more relaxed than it had been in the past.

10.

Eclipse

THERE is no question that Brando's star began to wane after *Mutiny on the Bounty,* during the five years after *The Appaloosa.* His slackening box-office appeal was underscored by a 1968 *Variety* survey that showed that his last six films had earned total receipts of only $9.6 million—an average of $1.6 million per picture. It was obvious that Brando's movies were not even recouping production costs. And things were to get worse.

A number of factors contributed to the decline in Brando's popularity. Not the least of them was his lack of interest in whether the roles he played would enhance his popularity with audiences. Brando seemed much more concerned with doing pictures that challenged him artistically or presented what he considered an important social message. Sometimes, too, he apparently chose to make a film for strictly financial reasons. Kazan once commented, "Some actors play a scene to promote themselves to an audience, for what the scene can do for them. They think, 'I've got to make them pity me here.' Not Brando. He doesn't want the audience to like or not like him. He just doesn't think about it."

Another factor contributing to Brando's decline was the lack of promotion that his pictures received during this period. Admittedly, *Bounty* opened amid a great deal of hoopla, but many of Brando's subsequent efforts went out almost unheralded by the movie industry.

Finally, a change in the public's taste was responsible for Brando's fading into the background. During the mid-sixties the youth culture began to make serious inroads into films. Surveys showed that the largest single segment of the movie audience was the under-thirty crowd. They wanted pictures that reflected their own image, that were "with it," that promoted their own values. And, as usual, Hollywood was quick to respond, with such pictures as *The Graduate, The Strawberry Statement, If,* and *Brewster McCloud.*

Somehow, Brando didn't quite fit into the new wave of pictures. First, and most obviously, he was too old. The choice parts were going to the young actors; the older players were used mainly as foils to the new generation of Americans. But there were other reasons. Brando's image of immense power and brooding sensitivity seemed somewhat old-fashioned. As Pauline Kael noted, there just weren't any roles for him. When Brando appeared in a film, the audience knew that he was too big for the character he was playing.

Too, Brando had been working in films for more than fifteen years. He had tried to confine his work to pictures with some redeeming qualities and had earned the enmity of a sizeable segment of the Hollywood establishment. When he saw that even worthwhile films had only a very limited effect in terms of social progress, he had sought to provide an example by way of his personal life. The effort probably had tired him, and seemingly he had grown just a bit cynical.

Many observers wondered what Brando's fate would be as a new generation of stars made its way to the top. Would he, like many has-beens, make a series of potboilers, drop into guest slots on television programs, appear in a few commercials, and finally vanish? Or would he, like Bette Davis and John Barrymore, spend his last days making parodies of himself?

Brando merely shrugged and said, "I feel as though I have come to the end of the line somewhere. I don't picture myself going on much further than six or seven years. I'll have to do something—one has to—but I don't know if it will be acting."

Brando was not without a few plans. One was to make a film called *Forbidden Dreams* based on an original screenplay by the French absurdist playwright Jean Genet. Tony Richardson, the English director, was to handle the production. But the film, which was ultimately titled *Mademoiselle,* starred French actress Jeanne Moreau and Italian actor Ettore Manni in the role that Brando had had his eye on.

Another project that never saw the light of day was a film version of Hochhuth's *The Deputy.* Anatole Litvak was scheduled to direct. Brando was so excited about the prospect that he confided, "I don't care if *The Deputy* doesn't make money. I'd do it for nothing."

Pennebaker was in no position to assist its troubled vice-president. The company had produced *The Fugitive Kind, Jacks,* and *Bedtime Story.* It had also made Gary Cooper's last film, *The Naked Edge,* and *Paris Blues,* starring Paul Newman, Joanne Woodward, Sidney Poitier, and Diahann Carroll. Unfortunately, none of the films had been big money-makers, and after the death of Marlon, Sr., the company ceased active operations.

Brando seemed willing to wait things out, but others were not content to let him rest on his laurels. In early 1966, he received a trans-Atlantic phone call offering him a part in an old-fashioned comedy. Brando accepted the role and later stated, "I would have acted in a phone booth for that man." Charlie Chaplin was "that man."

The picture was *A Countess from Hong Kong,* a story the seventy-six-year-old Chaplin had written in 1940 but had never had a chance to produce. He described it as a "romantic comedy—high, delicate comedy, I hope. And it's about real people; human, happy, touching, funny." *Countess* was to co-star Sophia Loren, who had impressed the venerable actor-director with her work in *Yesterday, Today and Tomorrow*. In addition, it would feature a song that Chaplin had written especially for the film. And, of course, there was always the chance that Charlie himself might appear in a small cameo role.

There is no question about the sincerity of Brando's respect for Chaplin. Over the years he had mentioned Chaplin as one of the greatest American actors. Once he had been asked to explain what acting was all about, and he had replied, "It's hard for me to articulate about acting. What can you say about a certain moment or expression? It's like Chaplin chewing a rose at the end of *City Lights.*"

The film was shot at the Pinewood Studios, outside London. It was the first film Chaplin had directed but not starred in since he had guided Adolphe Menjou and Edna Purviance in *A Woman of Paris* forty-three years before. Chaplin was clearly nervous about *Countess;* he and his stars worked a grueling seven-days-a-week schedule.

Almost everyone nearly broke down under the strain. Chaplin went over each scene line by line. He allowed a certain amount of improvisation by Brando and Loren. But he also knew exactly what he wanted, and he often stepped in to show one or the other of the stars how to play a scene.

To a question about how Brando and Loren were working out as a comedy team, Charlie replied, "Nobody in the film is being funny. I mean, coming on with the obvious intention of getting laughs. After all, you don't ask stars like Sophia and Marlon to clown."

Except for some playful kidding around with Sophia and a brief absence from the set due to his kidney condition, the star gave his director very little trouble. But Brando was not without his moments of doubt. "For the first few days," he said, "I thought I'd gone raving mad, Charlie had gone raving mad, and it was impossible. I can't do 'faces' and triple-takes—stuff like that. I was afraid both of us had made a big mistake. But then, suddenly, it all started to work. It was like chess—chess at ninety miles per hour."

Rare visitors on the set overheard Chaplin giving Brando such directions as "Marlon, when you pick up the glass at the door, don't pause. We have to keep up the choreography. No, no, Marlon. Too broad. Timing . . . timing . . . keep up the tension. There's a sag in your voice in the middle of that word. Get it out."

Slowly, painfully, each scene was polished. The work was unlike any other that Brando had done. He said while filming progressed, "My acting has always been— well, roomy. But this is different. It's a mosaic. We polish each piece, then fit it in place."

The critics were impressed by neither the overall design nor the brilliance of its bits and pieces. When *Countess* opened in London in January, 1967, they called Chaplin's eighty-first movie an "anachronism" that was "dull and ordinary." The fact that the film was Chaplin's first effort in color didn't make any difference. Nor did reviewers have much to say about Chaplin's brief appearance as a seasick steward in a short, richly comic scene.

Chaplin maintained that the so-called experts were "bloody idiots," but he wisely went to work cutting about twenty minutes from the film in an attempt to liven it up for the New York opening, which followed the London premier by three months.

Doubtless the editing improved the film. And the promotion afforded the American opening by Universal—complete with vintage autos and VIPs from Hollywood and government—was impressive. But the American critics were no more sympathetic than their counterparts overseas.

Crowther began his critique with the pronouncement that the film was a "painfully antique bedroom farce." *Countess* was so awful, he wrote, that he suspected briefly that Chaplin was putting everyone on. Noting that both Brando and Loren were weighed down with "ditch-water dull dialogue," he found the stars wasted in the effort. Referring to an old farce, *Up in Mabel's Room,* which had been popular decades previously, he suggested that the movie should have been titled "Up in Ogden's Room" (Brando's character being named Ogden in the movie).

Six months later Brando had to worry about another New York opening. Again he was playing a role that wasn't likely to win him many new fans. And for the first time since *Streetcar* he had to give over top billing to another film star. Nevertheless, a $75,000 salary plus 7 percent of the gross made *Reflections in a Golden Eye* worth his while. Of course, there was also the consideration that Carson McCuller's novel, on which the script was based, was a minor American classic.

The role of the homosexual Major Pendleton was originally to have gone to Montgomery Clift. Co-star Elizabeth Taylor, a close friend of the actor since they had appeared together in *A Place in the Sun,* had had Clift in mind for the part for some time. When Clift suffered a heart attack and died at the age of forty-five, Taylor was disconsolate. She also found herself without a leading man.

Brando had known Richard Burton for some years, having met him during one of his many visits to England. The fiery, poetry-spouting actor evidently appealed to Brando; not the least of Burton's attractions was his talent as a stage actor.

The feeling was mutual. Commenting later on Brando's ability, Burton said, "He constantly surprises me— he's the only one who does." Brando and Burton began to see each other whenever their busy schedules permitted. Later, after Burton and Taylor were married, Brando was an occasional visitor in their home.

Taking this into consideration, the choice of Brando for *Reflections in a Golden Eye* was a logical one. He was the best American actor around. Taylor and Burton had seen him do his Southern gentleman act in *Sayonara* and other films, and they were more than a little interested in seeing what he could make of the role of Major Pendleton.

Under the direction of veteran John Huston, shooting began in Rome at the studio of Dino De Laurentis. There were rumors of arguments between Taylor and Brando, but these were largely the invention of journalists desperate for some gossip about the production.

Later, the location switched to Mitchell Field on

Long Island, New York. Huston needed the feel of an army base for the picture, and he liked the fact that uniformed extras could be picked up for the asking. In addition, difficulties had arisen over the script, and the director and his writers wanted to be close to Carson McCullers, then gravely ill in Nyack, New York.

Curiously enough, despite the talent assembled for the film (Brian Keith and Julie Harris added commendable performances to those of Taylor and Brando), it was almost totally ignored by the critics. Perhaps the tale about what goes on behind the scenes in an army camp was too sordid. The plot included adultery, homosexuality, fetishism, and sado-masochism. Not surprisingly, the picture earned a "C" (Condemned) rating from the Catholic Church.

Pauline Kael was one of the few who risked a long and thoughtful review. Her piece in the *New Yorker,* though, was not overly complimentary at what the script-writers had done to McCuller's novel, and she found Taylor uneven. Her praise for Brando was quite lavish, calling him a great actor. Noting that Brando's characterization of the impotent, homosexual major doesn't always work, she added: "When it does, Brando shows how good he can be." Singling out a scene where Brando pats cold cream on his face and preens before a mirror in preparation for meeting a young lover, she said that it was so powerful and ghastly that, ". . . some members of the audience invariably cut themselves off from him by laughter."

Crowther's criticism of the work followed similar lines. He felt that the script didn't do justice to the novel and that it also failed to jell as a piece of drama. Crowther's major interest was in the way the roles were portrayed by the principals. In his estimation, the men came off better than the women. Taylor was too shrill, he wrote, and Harris too flat. On the other hand, he called Keith "surprisingly skillful" and gauged Brando's performance as "devastating."

Regardless of its critical and financial failure, *Reflections in a Golden Eye* is one of Brando's most important films and one that is significant in movie history. It is the first film to present a major star in the role of a homosexual. Kael commented that there probably wasn't another big name in Hollywood at that time who would have touched the part. *Reflections* opened up an area of contemporary life that had previously been taboo on the screen. Without the film, *The Boys in the Band* might have waited in the wings for quite a few more years than was the case before it was finally produced.

During this period, Brando became a kind of secret jet-setter, bouncing around the world whenever the whim struck him. One of his favorite stopping-off places was Tatieroa, a small atoll located about twenty-five miles north of Tahiti. He purchased the South Sea retreat in 1966 with hopes of setting up a kind of artistic-intellectual colony. Later, as we shall see, the island was to become of interest to him in terms of his environmental concerns.

Brando was also a frequent visitor to the country home of his sister outside Mundelein, Illinois. Every so often the local paper would get word that Brando had been seen entering the town's drugstore or hardware store. The editor would dutifully send a reporter out to see what was up. But the journalist's efforts were usually to no avail. Brando's family and friends kept him well protected from the press. On one occasion a luckless photographer waited in the auditorium of the local junior high school for an entire evening, having received a tip that Brando would show up for a performance of his niece in a school play. The photographer never got a shot of the star, although the kids later swore up and down that Brando had been in the audience.

In 1967 Brando and two friends toured parts of the Middle East and Africa. The group met in Switzerland, where Brando had been staying at the Swiss chalet of the Burtons.

They then flew to the small republic of Dahomey on the western coast of Africa, where Brando did a bit of work on an upcoming film. From there they went to Ghana, staying for a time with Franklin Williams, the American ambassador. Shortly afterward, they made their way to Cairo, where they met Ambassador Lucius D. Battle. The four-week trip ended with a brief tour of the Mediterranean area.

Brando at the time was involved with a film called *Burn!*. It had given him and Italian director Gillo Pontecorvo trouble almost from the beginning, and its history makes interesting reading. As Vincent Canby remarked in his *New York Times* review when the film finally opened in late 1970, "In the course of the production, *Burn!* turned into a kind of mini-*Cleopatra.*"

The film was originally titled *Queimada* (Portuguese for "burned"). Director Pontecorvo—the man behind the highly successful pseudo-documentary *Battle of Algiers* —had high hopes for the venture when he began filming in the old fortress city of Cartagena, Colombia. Pontecorvo, an admitted Communist, had himself written the story of the exploitation of black colonials. The film would show how one Western capitalist power after another helped to sow the seeds of a black revolution in a fictitious South American country. The director wanted the authenticity of the location in Colombia, but he soon realized that the spot was too primitive for his purposes. Some of his cast members came down with tropical diseases, and production was slowed. Ironically, there were also rumors of labor troubles, which could have proven embarrassing.

The location was therefore switched to Dahomey, and Brando took some time out from his vacation there to do some preliminary shooting.

Later, Pontecorvo wasn't satisfied with the first rushes. Retakes were scheduled, and more delays were encountered. Tempers flared under the relentless African sun, and before long the picture was far behind schedule. Needless to say, the budget was shot.

When the film was finally completed, it was quite a bit too long. The director sent it to an editor, who chopped out twenty minutes.

The next problem was finding a distributor. Finally, largely because of the reputation Pontecorvo had established with *The Battle of Algiers* and the fact that Brando was starring, United Artists agreed to release and distribute the film in America.

The studio didn't do much for *Burn!* as far as promotion was concerned. Pauline Kael, commenting in her *New Yorker* review on the lack of advance notice the film received, felt that United Artists had underestimated the picture's drawing power. With its "heavy" message about racial injustice and its revolutionary fervor, Kael maintained that *Burn!* was just the kind of film young moviegoers would have flocked to see—if only they had known about it.

Kael herself found the film exciting. Though she felt that Brando played his role a bit broadly—sometimes with comic effect—she excused the star on the grounds that a heavier portrait would have turned the picture into a Grade B melodrama.

Canby, after noting a few shortcomings in the direction, stated, "I must add that I wasn't bored by the film for even a minute. Furthermore, Mr. Brando is worth watching under almost any circumstances, and you should enjoy seeing him here, using that Fletcher Christian accent and, towards the end of the film, looking very much like the late Ernest Hemingway, a tired and tragic hero whom life has somehow double-crossed."

In general, however, the picture suffered from lack of interest on the part of critics. Kauffmann in the *New Republic* called it "carelessly made" and didn't comment on Brando's performance. Arthur Knight was no more enthusiastic and found the film's star "flaccid and dull."

During the same period in which he was involved in *Burn!*, Brando also found time for a bit of sheer film fun. When it was announced that a movie was to be made of *Candy,* Terry Southern's best-selling sex saga, the public was intrigued, to say the least. Could it be done? Brando was one of those elected to do the impossible.

The person responsible for getting Brando involved in the unfortunate mess that screenwriter Buck Henry tried to fashion from the Terry Southern-Mason Hoffenberg production was Christian Marquand, a former actor. Marquand, a native of France, had played opposite Bardot in *And God Created Woman.* Brando had befriended him during one of his trips to Paris years before. It was Marquand's idea to fill the picture with top stars in cameo roles. Did Brando have any ideas for the choice role of the mad poet?

Brando thought he knew just the right bloke for the part: Richard Burton, his old Bardic buddy.

Burton didn't seem too keen on the idea when Brando first approached him. He felt overworked, and he and Liz wanted to take it easy for a while. But reportedly Brando convinced him that he could combine business with pleasure. The film would be shot near Rome.

There'd be a lot of exciting people around—Walter Matthau, Ringo Starr (as the demented Mexican gardener),
John Huston, and Brando himself, to name a few. Finally, the Welshman decided to go along with the idea.

Reporters had a tough time getting any advance information out of the cast or production crew. When questioned on what direction the movie would take, screenwriter Buck Henry answered, "Every one conceivable
away from the book." And how was *Candy* going to
end? None of the actors seemed to know, and Henry
admitted, "We're keeping it a secret from them."

About the only thing reporters came away with was
the legend on a huge sign that Brando and other cast
members had erected in the Italian countryside near the
shooting location: "Save Our Republic—Impeach Earl
Warren!" All in all, the company of *Candy* was probably
the zaniest bunch of picture people to gather on the
Italian soil since Bogart, Lorre, Jennifer Jones, and Truman Capote had filmed *Beat the Devil* there some years
earlier.

The critics definitely were not amused when the picture premiered in December, 1968. Renata Adler, in her
new role as the *New York Times* film critic, led the pack
in calling *Candy* "faithful in dreary spirit to the best-
selling novel." She continued, "The movie, directed by
Christian Marquand, manages to compromise, by its relentless, crawling, bloody lack of talent, almost anyone
who had anything to do with it." She had this to say for
Brando and Burton: "Richard Burton, as a poet-seducer,
gives a firm, delighted, irrefutable demonstration of his
lack of any comic talent whatsoever . . . . Marlon Brando, as a Jewish Guru . . . is less unendurable because one
is glad to see him on the screen, in anything."

The best of the major reviewers, mercifully, didn't
bother to comment.

During the next two years, Brando was to work on

two other movies that added nothing to his reputation. Made during the darkest period of his career, it is ironic that both *The Night of the Following Day* and *The Nightcomers* made inadvertent references to the almost total eclipse that now beset him.

The first of them—*The Night of the Following Day*— was a tense and unjustly underrated adventure yarn that brought Brando and Rita Moreno together again—professionally, not romantically. Based on a novel called *The Snatchers,* it tells the story of three men and a woman who kidnap a rich girl, then fall out and kill one another after the ransom has been paid. Some local reviewers maintained that the film was the best Brando had done in years. Only *Time* among the major media took notice, confining its remarks on Brando to his appearance in long, blond hair.

The second of Brando's two "nocturnal" films, *The Nightcomers,* was made in England in the early part of 1971. Using the famous Henry James novel *The Turn of the Screw* as a jumping off point, it chronicles the events just prior to the time that the book begins. In the James chiller an impressionable and imaginative young governess takes over the care of two children—only to find them strangely corrupted. Literary critics have wondered whether her discovery is due to her own psychological quirks or because she is a perceptive observer.

In the original story the governess keeps seeing the ghostly figures of the former valet, Peter Quint, and the children's previous governess, Miss Jessel. The movie, which earned an "R" rating, dispels the Jamesian ambiguity by showing how the insidious Quint and his secret mistress, Miss Jessel, affected the children.

The fact that the *New York Times* carried only one review of the film—following its premier at the Venice

Film Festival in October, 1971—indicates how low Brando's stock had fallen. In that piece, by one of the paper's overseas correspondents, only the details of the plot are covered. Brando's name doesn't even appear!

Produced by one of the newer independent production companies, Scimitar Productions (founded by Elliott Kransner, J. Kanter, and Alan Ladd, Jr.), the film didn't find an American distributor for almost six months. And when it did, Avco-Embassy wasn't too excited about its prospects. There was enough sex and sadism in *The Nightcomers* to warrant the restricted rating it had earned. But the film had been done as a nineteenth-century costume piece (Brando wore long hair tied back in a Patrick Henry pigtail), and the decadence was presented in a highly intellectual framework. Hoping to find a propitious time for its release, the distributors delayed the film's premier until spring, 1972.

The strategy didn't help. When *The Nightcomers* opened in major cities across the United States, it didn't raise a ripple. In some cities it lasted only a week at the first-rate houses and then dropped from sight; in others, it opened at the secondary houses as part of a double feature and never made the rounds of the neighborhood theaters.

One Chicago distribution representative commented about the failure of the film, "It's no surprise to me. Nobody wants to see that guy anymore. As a matter of fact, I don't think any of his pictures have made money for the past ten years."

In some ways this box-office apathy was the price Brando paid for his quest for anonymity. He was staying away from Hollywood—his last four pictures had been primarily European productions. And Film City has never been gracious to those who desert it.

Brando, however, didn't realize just how low his profile had become. In December, 1968, he had just boarded a flight in Los Angeles on his way to Miami when a chance remark caused a brouhaha. As the stewardess came down the aisle to make sure her first-class passengers were comfortable before takeoff, a man in dark glasses, wearing his long hair in a pigtail, casually asked her if he was on the flight for Cuba.

The flustered young woman dutifully reported the incident to the captain. In turn, he radioed the tower for a conference. As passengers aboard the flight grumbled about the delay, it was finally decided best not to take any chances. Airline officials clambered aboard the plane to escort the suspected hijacker back to the terminal.

The man offered no resistance. In fact, he seemed to be enjoying the whole thing. Inside the terminal an official took one look at the suspect and gasped, "My God, it's Marlon Brando!"

The official offered to return him to the plane immediately, but Brando politely refused. He probably felt that enough fuss had been generated to alert his fellow passengers to his identity.

Another incident that showed how people had forgotten Brando also occurrred on an airplane. As the actor leaned back to relax during a transcontinental flight, the young man next to him kept fidgeting with a battered suitcase, trying to engage him in conversation. Brando feigned sleep for a while, then decided to hear the youth out.

"Look, I suppose you won't believe this, but I'm a fugitive from justice," the young man said furtively.

Brando seemed unimpressed.

"No, I'm telling the truth. I just robbed a savings and loan and am on my way out of the country," the young man pressed.

Though Brando reportedly feigned indifference, his co-passenger continued to try to convince him. Finally, unable to get a rise out of the star, he eased open his suitcase and showed a glimpse of neatly stacked bills. Again, Brando turned away to gaze out the window.

But minuted later, he excused himself to go to the bathroom. On his way, he informed the stewardess of what he had discovered. She told the captain, who notified Los Angeles. When the plane landed, the authorities were waiting at the ramp as the passengers departed. They quickly pulled the self-destructive robber to one side and commandeered his suitcase. Brando walked by while they were frisking him; one of the airline officials nodded to him and said, "Thanks, Mr. Brando." The would-be Dillinger did a double-take and stood with his mouth hanging open.

Not everyone in Hollywood had forgotten Brando, however. Elia Kazan wanted him for the film version of his best-selling novel, *The Arrangement,* in 1968. Brando looked over the script, then decided against it. Perhaps it would have been nice to work with his old friend again; but that would mean that Brando would have to go to Hollywood, and he seemed to hate the idea. He told Kazan that he was devoting his time to the civil rights movement and other causes. Besides, he preferred working in Europe. Later, Kirk Douglas accepted the role and failed to turn it into a money-maker.

Feelers for new roles kept reaching Brando sporadically as he bided his time. One after another, he turned them down. Then, early in 1970, somebody made him an offer he couldn't refuse.

11.

Comes the Don

O NE DAY, Mario Puzo, the author of *The Godfather,* was basking in his new-found glory as a best-selling, honest-to-God successful writer and casually leafing through a newspaper when he read something that probably almost gave him a heart attack. A skillful and dedicated writer who had written the book solely to make money, Puzo knew that Paramount was considering making a movie of his baby. But, evidently thinking back on all the writers whom Hollywood had done in over the years, he wasn't overly concerned about Paramount's approach to *The Godfather*—as long as he wasn't involved.

But the article he was reading seemed to change his mind in a flash. The Armenian comedian Danny Thomas had let it be known that he would like to get the role of Don Vito Corleone, the Godfather.

As Puzo later stated in *The Godfather Papers,* he had

always had very definite ideas about who should play that role. So, through a mutual friend, he obtained the address of the star he'd had in mind. He wrote the star a letter; shortly afterward, he received a phone call and immediately recognized the distinctive voice of Marlon Brando on the other end of the line.

During the discussion that followed, Brando told Puzo that he had not read the book and had little hope that Paramount would consider giving him the part. Unless the picture had a strong director who insisted on hiring him, it was probably a hopeless case, he said. Puzo found Brando polite and friendly but somewhat uninterested.

At the time, the author wasn't aware that Paramount had all but scrapped the idea of doing the movie. The studio had just made a movie with Kirk Douglas called *The Brotherhood;* the film had bombed, and Paramount was not about to sink any money into another film in what seemed to be an unpopular and all-but-dead genre. Only when *The Godfather* went on to become a smash hit, chalking up sixty-seven weeks on the *New York Times* best-seller list, did the studio heads revise their thinking. The movie *had* to be made.

Puzo was approached to do the script; he negotiated on price and finally agreed. After establishing himself in a plush office at the studio, he played a bit of tennis and saw old friends for a few weeks. Then he had a conference about the picture with the studio heads.

Present at the first conference were Al Ruddy, the producer of the picture, Robert Evans, Paramount's reputedly hard-nosed production chief, and other biggies. The first meeting was evidently designed to be a kind of pep talk to build Puzo's enthusiasm for the film. But during the discussion that followed, the group realized that there just might be some problems with the production. For one thing, they had no director. Puzo would be writing more or less blind, since most directors sign only after approving the script. So from the start there was a good possibility that when Paramount did get a director, a revision of Puzo's script might be called for.

In addition, the front office had widely different ideas about who should star in the film. Ruddy wanted Robert Redford for the role of Michael Corleone, the youngest son and eventual heir of the Don, and Puzo felt uneasy. When he suggested that Brando was just right for the role of the Don, Puzo got the impression that the executives all hoped that he would confine his interest in the project to the writing.

Work on the script dragged on until 1971. When it was finished, the picture still had no director. The post had been offered to Costa Gavras, the man who had directed *Z*. But he turned the job down on the ground that as a foreigner he was unqualified to direct so American a film. Finally, the studio came up with the name of Francis Ford Coppola. He was young, of Italian background, and had just suffered two previous film failures. The studio heads figured that Coppola would be close to the picture yet would be controllable.

The problems of casting still had not been solved. When Puzo met Coppola, he again suggested Brando for the role of the Don. Though the author forewarned Coppola that everyone else was against it, the director liked the idea. Puzo at first felt that the big-bearded director was just a jovial Italian kid. He soon found out that he was mistaken. Coppola could be very tough when he wanted to be—and he really wanted Marlon Brando. In the end, over all the objections of the front office, he got what he was after.

It took some work on Coppola's part to persuade Paramount to hire Brando. Between the first conference with Puzo and the time Coppola was hired, almost every prestigious actor over thirty-five had been considered by the studio. Among them were George C. Scott, Laurence Olivier, and Italian producer Carlo Ponti, husband of Sophia Loren. Waiting in the wings was Frank Sinatra, who reportedly told Coppola that although he hated the book, he'd do a favor for the young director. Movie people were not the only ones after the role. According to *Time* magazine, such well-known figures as the San Francisco lawyer Melvin Belli said they would like to take a crack at the role.

Meanwhile, Coppola and Puzo kept plugging for Brando. When the director first made the suggestion, there was outright hostility to the idea. Biding his time, Coppola made it again, and this time the studio heads agreed—but with the stipulation that the seasoned star would have to undergo a screen test for the part!

The idea may have appealed to Brando's sense of the ridiculous—or possibly to his competitive spirit. In any case, according to one source, he beat the studio to the punch, with the aid of Coppola, by submitting a videotape of his interpretation of the role before the demand became official.

One evening Brando transformed himself into the Don while Coppola recorded the whole process with his camera. First the actor slicked back his hair, streaked it with gray, and put some black shoe polish under his eyes. Then he stuffed tissue paper in his cheeks and nostrils. Finally, he picked up a small espresso coffee cup, lit a crooked Italian stogie, and began pacing around the room, muttering to himself in an Italian accent. Coppola exclaimed later, "God, it was just like my uncle Louie!"

When the people from the front office at Paramount heard the tape, they almost fell out of their executive chairs. Stanley Jaffe, president of Paramount, had previously told the director and the production staff, "I must tell you that under no circumstances will Marlon Brando appear in *The Godfather!* And, as president, I no longer wish to waste the company's time even discussing it." But Brando's brief performance convinced the studio heads that he would make an excellent Don.

Still, despite their enthusiasm for Brando's interpretation of the title role, the Paramount executives were cautious about the contract they offered. Reportedly, Brando would get a relatively meager $50,000 salary. Secondly, though he would receive a percentage of the net profits, he would have to guarantee with his own money that the film would not be delayed in any way by his own actions.

Explaining why he had pushed so hard for the older star, Coppola later said, "He meant a lot to me when I was eighteen and just starting. I finally came to the conclusion that we should get the greatest actor in the world and say to him: 'Create the Godfather for us.' "

In addition, Coppola told the studio heads that Brando would inspire the kind of awe among his fellow actors in the film that the character of the Don demanded.

Given the fact that Brando beat Paramount to the punch by offering his own screen test and furthermore agreed to the studio's conditions, his apparent initial lack of interest in the movie obviously had changed to fascination between the time he first spoke to Puzo and the time when Coppola approached him. Brando later told Shana Alexander in an interview for *Life* magazine that he became intrigued by the book and movie because the Mafia seemed "so American." When he thought about the way the Godfather and his organization eliminated their opponents, he was reminded of McNamara, President Johnson, and Dean Rusk. The film, he suggested, made a comment on our society in that the values of the Mafia—which place policy and money above human life—parallel those of big business and big government.

Brando was undoubtedly pleased about landing the role, but he was not without worries during this period. His children in Tahiti and Mexico seemed to be doing all right. But the actor must have experienced a growing concern for his oldest son, Christian. According to some sources, Anna had attempted suicide in 1970. Rumor had it that she was still rather shaky, though she was attempting to get back on her feet. And Christian was back with Anna.

There were difficulties with the movie as well, centered on finding Brando a supporting cast. John Marley and Richard Conte, who had been considered for the role of Don Corleone, had agreed to take smaller parts. But the Don was still without heirs. Such suggestions as Robert Redford, Warren Beatty, and Jack Nicholson were ruled out because Coppola wanted less familiar faces. Finally, after numerous screen tests and arguments, he was able to cast Al Pacino as Michael, James Caan as Sonny, and Robert Duval as Tom Hagen. A big surprise for everyone was Coppola's selection of singer Morgana King for the role of the mother. Certain parts were not cast until Coppola was on location. For example, he spotted former wrestler Lenny Montana on the streets of New York and felt that he was just right for the part of Luca Brasi, the cold-blooded killer.

There were also problems about the budget and location. At first the movie was afforded a modest $1 million budget. It was to be a quickie, using on-location shots in St. Louis. Coppola, however, had big ideas about his movie and wasn't satisfied with just going through the paces. He was thinking in terms of authentic period costumes, cars, and other props, which would boost expenses significantly. Coppola also wanted to shoot the film in New York City and Long Island—where costs were bound to be double, if not triple.

Coppola's plans for the film led to a furious debate with the producers. But the director stuck to his guns, and eventually the producers gave in. Coppola spent about $6 million of their money before he was finished.

Almost as soon as the studio heads announced that they were going ahead with the project, trouble developed on other fronts. As had been the case with *On the Waterfront*, there were vague threats that there would be labor trouble, and it was hinted that the producers might find themselves in hot water when they moved their equipment on location. And there were more personal threats. Producer Al Ruddy's car was found riddled with bullet holes one morning. Later there was a bomb threat at the offices of Gulf & Western, Paramount's parent company.

The Italian-American Civil Rights League objected strongly to the projected film and held a benefit in New York to raise a war chest for their cause. The league also contacted stars of Italian descent in an effort to convince them that it would not be in their interests to work in the picture. Vic Damone, for example, who was originally offered the role of Johnny Fontane, declined after thinking it over, stating that the film would harm the image of Italian-Americans. And even Coppola found himself being stopped on the street by strangers who asked, "How can a nice Italian boy like you make a movie like that?"

Ruddy tried to head off trouble by meeting with the heads of the league. He reportedly offered to donate the proceeds of the film's opening night to the group. Studio executives at Paramount and board members of Gulf

& Western wouldn't hear of it, however, and Ruddy had to back off.

Trying another tack, Ruddy was able to make peace with the group. In one shrewd move he agreed to strike any references to *Mafia* or *Cosa Nostra* from the script if the league would back off. As Puzo later commented, it was a nice piece of bargaining since the words had never been in the script in the first place.

To lend his peace offering a more personal touch, Ruddy agreed to hire some friends of the league's most vociferous opponent of the movie. Thus did Gianni Russo, a Las Vegas nightclub emcee, get the role of Carlo, the double-dealing son-in-law of the Godfather.

The vague threats of labor troubles and other difficulties never materialized, and the cooperation of the league paid off. Some of those hired through connections with the group acted as consultants, advising Coppola on the ways of the Mafia. (Coppola also had help from former New York detectives E. Egan and S. Grosso, both of whom had served in similar capacities on *Bullitt* and *The French Connection.)*

The big question, once everything else was settled, was how Brando would behave on the set. He had his own money on the line, but then the studio felt one never knew with a guy like Brando. Suppose he didn't like the lines written for him or didn't agree with Coppola on how key scenes should be played? Would the producers have another *Mutiny* on their hands?

Their fears were soon dispelled. Just before shooting began, Coppola arranged a cast party at an Italian restaurant in Manhattan. Though Brando had worked with Duval on *The Chase,* many members of the cast had never met before, and it was a tense evening at first. Then Brando stepped forward, picked up a bottle of wine, and started the festivities by filling everyone's glass. It was as though he was already playing the role of the Don to his family of fellow actors.

On location, Brando continued to carry out the mock relationship. Pacino, Caan, and Duval were treated as if they were Brando's real sons. He clowned with them, gave them advice, and lent a spirit of enthusiasm to the whole project. Long known for his love of high jinks, he encouraged his "sons" to engage in such ludicrous pranks as "mooning" (baring one's behind in public). Caan later recalled that one of his best "moons" had taken place on New York's Second Avenue while Duval was driving him to work. They spotted Brando's car up ahead; when they pulled up beside him at a light, Caan dropped his pants and thrust his buttocks out the window. "Brando damn near fell out of the car with laughter," he related.

Perhaps the "son" whom Brando helped the most was Al Pacino. From an Italian background himself, Pacino quickly appreciated the depth and genuineness of the older actor's characterization. Later, he recalled that in one scene near the end of the movie, "I felt like I was talking to my grandfather." And throughout the filming Pacino found Brando "warm and understanding."

Coppola soon added his praise to that of other directors who had worked with Brando and had seen the lengths to which he would go to develop and maintain a character. The elaborate makeup for the Don was created under Brando's direction. To achieve the effect that he was hard-of-hearing toward the end of the picture, Brando stuffed toilet paper in his ears so that he actually had trouble hearing. Commenting on Brando's total commitment to the role of the Don, Coppola told a *Time* interviewer, "There was a full flush of intuition that Brando fused with his technique. If a herd of buffalo ran across the set, he'd react in character."

Possibly the only time that Brando stepped out of character was after filming the scene in which the God-father is gunned down by members of a rival mob. After it was over, the crowds that lined the New York street where the scene was filmed responded with a rousing, spontaneous cheer for his performance. He acknowledged it by waving and making a courtly bow.

Coppola was continually amazed by the inventive pieces of business that Brando came up with. One of these was the famous insertion of an orange peel in the Don's mouth during his death scene. Brando had played the same trick on his own children to frighten and delight them. The effect on the child with whom he was sharing the scene was perfect—first terror, then laughter. But it went deeper than that. Brando's momentary transformation into a grotesque monster was a metaphoric comment on the character of the Don.

There was no question that Brando was going to be back in the money—both literally and figuratively—when *The Godfather* opened on March 15, 1972, in five—count 'em, five!—first-class theaters in New York. The reviews of the picture and Brando's stunning performance were overwhelmingly favorable. Vincent Canby remarked,

> After a very long time, in too many indifferent or half-realized movies, giving performances that were occasionally becalmed but always more interesting than the material, Marlon Brando has finally connected with a character and a film that need not embarrass America's most complex, idiosyncratic film actor, nor those critics who have wondered in bossy print, whatever happened to him.

The response of the public was equally positive. A little more than a month after *The Godfather* opened, *Variety* predicted that the film could possibly gross as high as $75 million based on the initial box-office response. The following month, *Time* ran a spread on the film in its business section. *The Godfather,* said the article, had been a shot in the arm for the whole ailing movie industry, piling up receipts of $1 million a day. Noting that huge crowds waited for hours in front of the five houses featuring the film and that scalpers were getting up to $20 for a ticket, *Time* said *The Godfather* was a sure bet to gross $100 million and beat the all-time box-office champion, *Gone with the Wind.*

Of course, Brando profited—and will continue to profit—from the success of *The Godfather.* Some sources report that in addition to his advance, the star's percentage of the profits (2.5 percent of the first $10 million, 5 percent of the next $15 million, and 25 percent over $25 million) should total close to $16 million.

But as they say, money isn't everything. Just prior to the opening of *The Godfather* and during the first weeks of the film's run, Brando again probably found himself worrying about his oldest son, Christian. In 1971 a superior court had ruled that Christian would become a ten-month-a-year resident of the Ojai Valley School in southern California. During the summer, said the court, the boy would return to his mother. Brando would share custody of the boy while he was in school.

Almost a year later, school authorities reported the boy missing. Details of subsequent events are confused and sketchy, but it is reported that both Brando and Anna hired detectives to locate the boy and bring him back. Rumors circulated that Christian had been kidnapped while on a fishing trip in Baja, California, but Brando advised that there was nothing to worry about. His version was that his son merely had gone on a scuba-diving excursion with some friends.

In the meantime, Anna proceeded to Calexico, California, where she was supposed to meet a detective and

Christian. When her son failed to show up, she boarded a Greyhound bus with a friend and started back to Los Angeles. Distraught over her son's whereabouts, she evidently began to drink; she was arrested for creating a disturbance on the bus in El Centro.

A few days later, Christian entered the United States via Calexico with Brando's detective, J. Armes. Armes reported that Christian had been found in a fishing camp in Baja. One of the local fishermen told the detective that Anna had offered him $10,000 to return the boy to her.

Up until this time, Brando had been sharing custody of Christian with Anna. After the Baja incident, the star went to court to obtain full control of his son. Matters were complicated in the following weeks by the fact that Brando, prior to the hearing, found himself temporarily marooned on a small island near Tahiti when he and friends went out for a day's sailing.

A bitter and lengthy court fight ensued. Anna sought public sympathy via stories in the movie magazines— "I'll Never Let You Go!"—which were designed to show her attachment to the boy.

In the end, Brando won out. A court in Santa Monica, California, ruled in his favor, granting him sole custody of his son.

Naturally this posed problems for Christian's father. At the time of the Santa Monica decision he was on location in Paris for a film written and directed by the brilliant Italian Bernardo Bertolucci. Brando packed his son's suitcases and brought him to the City of Lights, where the star planned to enroll Christian in school.

The picture with Bertolucci, still waiting for release at this writing, promises to be another interesting effort. The much-praised Italian, who stunned critics with his version of Moravia's novel *The Conformist*, has been a lifelong fan of Brando. He first saw the star in *Viva Zapata!* when he was ten years old. Since his father was a film critic in Parma, Italy, Bertolucci had access to free passes; he saw *Zapata* and other Brando movies over and over till he had almost memorized them.

At first, Bertolucci had rejected the idea of featuring well-known actors in *Last Tango in Paris.* He felt that the effects of the first pangs of passion would be more believable when registered on unknown faces. But after viewing the paintings of Francis Bacon, the contemporary English master best known for portraits that project the anguish of a silent scream, Bertolucci changed his mind.

"I thought of Brando then," he told an interviewer. "He is the only actor whose face can express the same subconscious Freudian despair I saw in those paintings."

Brando was on location for *The Godfather* when he received a letter from Bertolucci asking him to consider the role of a middle-aged American who becomes involved with a youthful French girl. Brando had heard very good things about the Italian's films—especially *The Conformist.* In his spare time he went to see the film for himself; shortly afterward, he arranged a meeting with Bertolucci in Los Angeles. Later, the two met in Paris, where the final details of the arrangement were worked out. Brando's stock had risen as a result of *The Godfather;* he was able to obtain a reported $300,000 plus a percentage of the box-office receipts.

Still, one wonders if *Last Tango,* interesting and artistically significant though it might prove, will carry Brando to new heights in popularity. There will be no other well-known actors in the film. The other main roles will be handled by twenty-year-old Maria Schneider (daughter of popular French actor Danel Gelin) and Jean-Pierre Léaud, Truffaut's protégé. And Bertolucci's films have never generated the kind of popular interest that guarantees huge financial returns.

Of course, Brando needn't worry about such things— if, indeed, he ever did to any great extent. Money is obviously not a problem for him; popularity has always seemed a dubious honor that he has treated with a mixture of aloofness and irony. Nevertheless, at the age of forty-eight he may be facing the biggest problem of his life—one that has plagued him in one form or another since he first decided to jump up on a stage and project his own unique blend of power, sensitivity, artistry, and humanistic concern. A myriad of options is now, more than ever, before him. The question remains: in what direction will the dynamic and self-driven star move next? The Don is going to be a tough act to follow.

12.

Quo Vadis, Brando?

Earlier in his career, Brando once admitted that although he often found himself working up great enthusiasm for one project or another, he could rarely sustain it for more than several minutes. This characteristic has led to a rather impulsive, if not hectic, lifestyle, which has kept his fans and friends wondering just who he really is. Is he a dilettante, a gadfly, a professional iconoclast? How sincere is he about the values and causes he champions?

Such questions seem unique to Brando. Other Hollywood stars have led more outlandish lives, have had more uneven careers, and have espoused more unpopular causes without suffering from a tarnished image. Such popular figures as Frank Sinatra and George C. Scott can run the gamut of antisocial behavior without rousing more than token antagonism on the part of the media or the public. Paul Newman and Steve McQueen can make commercial potboilers without bitter recriminations from the critics. And Jack Nicholson and Peter Fonda can espouse the legalization of marijuana and still come up winners at the box office.

Perhaps Brando's peculiar vulnerability to criticism is due, as Pauline Kael once implied, to his towering talent. One expects so much more from him because he is so outstanding—a once-in-a-lifetime actor.

It is also possible to attribute the public's on-again-off-again romance with Brando to psychological and generational causes.

Early in Brando's career, when he was Hollywood's most visible and vociferous rebel, he exhibited certain self-destructive characteristics that came back to haunt him the rest of his career. He refused to play the Hollywood game, and many people both in and out of the film establishment were never willing to forgive and forget. He admitted later that as a young man he had a rather precious attitude about his own integrity. But this admission didn't do much to curb the resentment he had provoked as a youth.

Another of Brando's controversial statements reflects the values and problems of a whole generation of Americans: "I'm the Horatio Alger story . . . I'm the kid from the middle-income bracket who never finished high school and went the route of individualism—and made it. I've done what my country told me to do: 'Go on, kid, you can do it—that's what we want you to do.' But you know, it's a fraud and a gyp. . . . It's the biggest disappointment."

The idea that they must constantly be *doing* something was that of a generation of Americans from their earliest years. If one didn't have a specific goal or program by the time one entered high school, alarmed parents were liable to ask, "Well, what are you going to be—a bum?"

This kind of generational guilt seemed to plague Brando far into his adult life. He evidently couldn't merely swing with whatever came up. He had to be doing something important. Brando's apparent uneasiness was exacerbated by his country's values: a sizable number of Americans consider actors to be little better than frivolous drones. Acting? Why, that isn't work; it's play!

Brando's role in the creation of some of the most outstanding films in American cinematic history presumably just wasn't enough for him. There had to be something more important. And the fact that he was so open and honest about his dissatisfaction didn't help matters. Fans and commentators who were suspicious of the star at first finally became bored with Brando's continual searching.

Recent interviews show that despite a deepened self-awareness and circumspect maturity, Marlon Brando's quest for meaning in his life is far from over. He may view the limitations of his art with detachment and even cynicism, but he is still a goal-oriented individual from another era.

One of Brando's latest projects involves his five-mile-square island retreat, Tatieroa. Brando advises that he won't be living alone there; nor does he consider the island a place to cop out. He hopes to establish a scientific community that will research ways of living "in this technological age without subscribing to its demands." Brando feels that "there must be a way of accomplishing things without turning to the industrial giants." The community on Tatieroa will—it is hoped—raise animals, trap methane gas from compost piles for power, and test other ways of obtaining power without harming the environment.

As to just who will populate this pollution-free paradise, Brando remains somewhat vague. At the present time, the island is uninhabited, but Brando hopes ultimately to attract an international group of technicians, artists—anyone who can contribute to the success of the enterprise.

Brando also has expressed an interest in making quasi-documentary films about such topics as pollution, aggression, and overpopulation. One project, which, as we have seen, he has been planning for years, concerns the plight of the American Indian.

Paradoxically, Brando no longer believes that films or the example of a famous person can do much to effect social change. To an interviewer for *Oui* magazine, the star admitted, "The fundamental aspects of human nature are inflexible. I don't think there's anything a person like myself can do. Christ, Buddha, Socrates, Nietzsche—these men were all great thinkers, and yet they did not bring about any fundamental changes in human nature."

As far as movies are concerned, he reflected, "People go to the cinema, they pay money, to have someone else act out their fantasies. They think it's a good film if the actors re-create their fantasies the way they visualize them. But if the performances contradict their feelings or if they are opposed to their view of life, they think it is a lousy picture."

One would suppose, given such an outlook, that Brando might simply drop out. But besides his plans for documentaries, he is interested in long-range projects that teach through example rather than preaching.

Though Brando may feel that his ability to further human progress is limited, there can be little doubt that he has had a far-reaching and lasting effect on the movies.

In terms of acting alone, Brando established a new style. It was unlike anything seen on the screen before and brought a new feeling of power and spontaneity to films. The actor has a host of imitators; such names as James Dean, Paul Newman, Steve McQueen, and Warren Beatty spring immediately to mind. But even among the newer stars—Dustin Hoffman, Robert Redford, and Jack Nicholson, to name a few—his influence cannot be underestimated.

In addition, the types of roles that Brando was willing to tackle expanded the horizon of filmmakers. For the most part, until Brando's arrival on the scene, stars demanded roles that would cast them in a sympathetic light and increase their popularity with adoring fans. Brando has from the beginning seemed to care less about protecting his image than he has about making worthwhile films. His detachment and unconcern led ultimately to the creation of the antihero motive—seen in *Hud* or *Carnal Knowledge*—in which the main character is often an out-and-out bastard.

When one considers Brando in relation to the rebel archetype—a genre he practically created—it can be seen that his example in this area moved far beyond the confines of the screen. Brando was viewed as an iconoclast not only in his characterizations but in real life as well. Again this quality had a profound effect on those stars who came after him. By insisting on script approval, standing up for his rights as an artist against the demands of a commercial industry, and showing others that it was possible to create their own production companies, he did much to break the stranglehold that the studios previously had exercised over their "properties." Further, through his example as an activist in social issues, he showed that it was possible (and proper) for stars to stand up for their beliefs. And, finally, his continual ridicule of such figures as Hedda Hopper and Louella Parsons helped to undercut the effect that gossip columnists had on his profession.

One achievement that has been consistently overlooked is Brando's ability to create a whole spectrum of screen portraits. Too often he is stereotyped as the Rebel or the Mumbler. But what about the wide differences among Kowalski in *Streetcar,* Sky Masterson in *Guys and Dolls,* Sakini in *The Teahouse of the August Moon,* Gruver in *Sayonara,* the two Christians of *The Young Lions* and *Mutiny on the Bounty,* Pendleton in *Reflections in a Golden Eye,* and Don Corleone in *The Godfather?* One need only ask what other star has risked himself in such a kaleidoscope of roles to appreciate Brando's talent—and courage.

Quite possibly he will need all the courage he can muster to meet the challenges that lie ahead. On a personal level, he probably will continue to have troubles with his first wife, Anna. Though Brando now has sole custody of his oldest son, Christian, it seems unlikely that the boy's mother will accept this state of affairs. Then, too, there is Christian himself and his half-brothers and sisters. Children have a way of becoming problems once they reach adolescence. Certainly Brando can expect his share of parental difficulties in the years to come.

On a public level Brando may also find himself in disrepute from time to time. As long as he continues to support such causes as the Black Panthers and the anti-war movement and involve himself with non-Caucasian women, he is bound to arouse the wrath of the more conservative segments of American society.

Nor are the less tolerant factions likely to be the only people to cast aspersions on Brando's character. The actor's mature outlook, his loss of idealism and cool detachment, may offend even those who look to him as a liberal spokesman. Many will doubtless interpret his plans to establish a pollution-free society on his South Sea island as a retreat from reality and social responsibility.

As far as Brando's career is concerned, there is no question that his best years may still lie ahead of him—regardless of his claims that his acting days are just about over. Even a hostile Hollywood cannot ignore his talent for long; he is just too good to be allowed to go out to pasture. And some of the biggest stars have done their most outstanding work after the age of forty. James Cagney, for example, was forty-three when he won the Academy Award for *Yankee Doodle Dandy*. Gary Cooper was over fifty when he got his Oscar for *High Noon*. And John Wayne had to wait until he was sixty-two before *True Grit* brought him the little golden statue.

It seems unlikely that Brando will be reduced to a series of character roles in the future. He is just too great and would overshadow any other actors he appeared with. A return to the stage is even more improbable. Brando seems too restless, too dynamic to limit himself to a role that could stretch on for an extended Broadway run. Besides, Brando never has particularly cared for New York as a place to live for more than a short time. There is also the problem of the dearth of worthwhile material. American playwrights for some time have failed to produce the kind of drama that could attract his interest.

But who can tell? There are still countless classical roles that are crying out for the Brando treatment. Early in Brando's career, a director commented that there was a Faust in the stormy young actor. That seems even more true today, after Brando has spent decades in pursuit of an ineffable ideal. Then there are the Shakespearian roles: Coriolanus, Macbeth, Lear, Brutus—the list seems almost endless. Or perhaps he might try something lighter to exercise what Crowther called Brando's "considerable talents as a farceur." Moliere springs to mind, as does Shaw.

In any event, the future for Marlon Brando is bound to be as surprising and unpredictable as his life and career up to this time. Whether he succeeds in establishing a model community on Tatieroa, follows through on any of the numerous other projects in which he has expressed interest, or continues to pick and choose choice parts that will carry him to new artistic heights, his actions are bound to shock, scandalize, amaze, and inspire both those who have followed his career in the past and a whole new generation of film-goers who are just beginning to appreciate him.

And with any luck he may finally succeed in satisfying his harshest and most persistent critic—Marlon Brando, himself.

Marlon Brando Filmography

1950

The Men
PRODUCED BY STANLEY KRAMER
RELEASED THROUGH UNITED ARTISTS
Directed by Fred Zinneman
Original screenplay by Carl Foreman

Ken Wilozek	Marlon Brando
Ellen	Teresa Wright
Dr. Brock	Everett Sloane
Norm	Jack Webb
Angel	Richard Erdman

1951

A Streetcar Named Desire
PRODUCED BY CHARLES K. FELDMAN
WARNER BROTHERS
Directed by Elia Kazan
Original screenplay by Tennessee Williams

Stanley Kowalski	Marlon Brando
Blanche du Bois	Vivien Leigh
Stella Kowalski	Kim Hunter
Mitch	Karl Malden
Steve	Rudy Bond
Pablo	Nick Dennis

209

1952

Viva Zapata!
PRODUCED BY DARRYL F. ZANUCK
TWENTIETH CENTURY-FOX
Directed by Elia Kazan
Original screenplay by John Steinbeck

Emiliano Zapata	Marlon Brando
Josefa Espejo	Jean Peters
Eufemio Zapata	Anthony Quinn
Fernando	Joseph Wiseman
Soldadera	Margo
Señora Espejo	Mildred Dunnock

1953

Julius Caesar
PRODUCED BY JOHN HOUSEMAN
METRO-GOLDWYN-MAYER
Directed by Joseph L. Mankiewicz

Mark Antony	Marlon Brando
Julius Caesar	Louis Calhern
Brutus	James Mason
Cassius	John Gielgud
Casca	Edmond O'Brien
Calpurnia	Greer Garson
Portia	Deborah Kerr
Marullus	George Macready

1953

The Wild One
PRODUCED BY STANLEY KRAMER
RELEASED THROUGH COLUMBIA PICTURES
Directed by Laslo Benedek
Screenplay by John Paxton

Johnny . . . . Marlon Brando
Kathie . . . . Mary Murphy
Chino . . . . Lee Marvin
Sheriff Singer . . . . Jay C. Flippen

1954

On The Waterfront
PRODUCED BY S.P. EAGLE (SAM SPIEGEL)
RELEASED THROUGH COLUMBIA PICTURES
Directed by Elia Kazan
Original screenplay by Budd Schulberg

Terry Malloy	Marlon Brando
Edie Doyle	Eva Marie Saint
Father Barry	Karl Malden
Johnny Friendly	Lee J. Cobb
Charley Malloy	Rod Steiger
Truck	Tony Galento
Barney	Abe Simon
Tillio	Tami Mauriello
Glover	Leif Erickson
Gillette	Marty Balsam

Desiree
PRODUCED BY JULIAN BLAUSTEIN
TWENTIETH CENTURY-FOX
Directed by Henry Koster
Screenplay by Daniel Taradash

Napoleon	Marlon Brando
Désirée	Jean Simmons
Josephine	Merle Oberon
Bernadotte	Michael Rennie
Joseph Bonaparte	Cameron Mitchell
Mme. Bonaparte	Cathleen Nesbitt
Mme. Tallien	Carolyn Jones

1955

Guys and Dolls
PRODUCED BY SAMUEL GOLDWYN
RELEASED THROUGH METRO-GOLDWYN-MAYER
Directed by Joseph L. Mankiewicz
Screenplay by Joseph L. Mankiewicz

Sky Masterson	Marlon Brando
Sarah Brown	Jean Simmons
Nathan Detroit	Frank Sinatra
Miss Adelaide	Vivian Blaine
Nicely-Nicely Johnson	Stubby Kaye
Harry the Horse	Sheldon Leonard
Society Max	George E. Stone
Arvid Abernathy	Regis Toomey

1956

The Teahouse of the August Moon
PRODUCED BY JACK CUMMINGS
METRO-GOLDWYN-MAYER
Directed by Daniel Mann
Screenplay by John Patrick

Sakini	Marlon Brando
Captain Fisby	Glenn Ford
Lotus Blossom	Machiko Kyo
Captain McLean	Eddie Albert
Colonel Purdy	Paul Ford

1957

Sayonara
PRODUCED BY WILLIAM GOETZ
WARNER BROTHERS
Directed by Joshua Logan
Screenplay by Paul Osborn

Major Gruver	Marlon Brando
Hana-ogi	Miiko Taka
Kelly	Red Buttons
Katsumi	Miyoshi Umeki
General Webster	Kent Smith
Bailey	James Garner
Nakamura	Ricardo Montalban

1958

The Young Lions
PRODUCED BY AL LICHTMAN
TWENTIETH CENTURY-FOX
Directed by Edward Dmytryk
Screenplay by Edward Anhalt

Christian	Marlon Brando
Noah	Montgomery Clift
Michael Whiteacre	Dean Martin
Hope Plowman	Hope Lange
Margaret Freemantle	Barbara Rush
Hardenberg	Maximilian Schell
Gretchen Hardenberg	May Britt
Private Faber	Sam Gilman

1960

The Fugitive Kind

PRODUCED BY MARTIN JUROW AND RICHARD A. SHEPHERD
RELEASED THROUGH UNITED ARTISTS
Directed by Sidney Lumet
Screenplay by Tennessee Williams and Meade Roberts

Val Xavier	Marlon Brando
Lady Torrance	Anna Magnani
Carol Cutrere	Joanne Woodward
Vee Talbott	Maureen Stapleton
Jabe Torrance	Victor Jory

1961

One Eyed Jacks

PRODUCED BY FRANK P. ROSENBERG FOR PENNEBAKER, INC.
RELEASED THROUGH PARAMOUNT PICTURES
Directed by Marlon Brando
Screenplay by Guy Trosper and Calder Willingham

Rio	Marlon Brando
Dad Longworth	Karl Malden
Louisa	Pina Pellicer
Maria	Katy Jurado
Bob Amory	Ben Johnson
Lon	Slim Pickens
Harvey	Sam Gilman

1962

Mutiny on the Bounty
PRODUCED BY AARON ROSENBERG
METRO-GOLDWYN-MAYER
Directed by Carol Reed and Lewis Milestone
Screenplay by Charles Lederer

Fletcher Christian . . . . Marlon Brando
William Bligh . . . . Trevor Howard
John Mills . . . . Richard Harris
Alexander Smith . . . . Hugh Griffith
Maimiti . . . . Tarita

1963

The Ugly American
PRODUCED BY GEORGE ENGLUND
RELEASED THROUGH UNIVERSAL PICTURES
Directed by George Englund
Screenplay by Stewart Stern

Harrison Carter MacWhite . . . . . . Marlon Brando
Deong . . . . Eiji Okada
Marion MacWhite . . . . Sandra Church
Homer Atkins . . . . Pat Hingle
Emma Atkins . . . . Jocelyn Brando

1964

Bedtime Story (King of the Mountain)
PRODUCED BY STANLEY SHAPIRO FOR PENNEBAKER, INC.
AND LANKERSHIM CO.
RELEASED THROUGH UNIVERSAL PICTURES
Directed by Ralph Levy
Screenplay by Stanley Shapiro and Paul Henning

Freddy .... Marlon Brando
Lawrence ..., ... David Niven
Janet .... Shirley Jones
Fanny Eubank .... Dody Goodman

1965

The Saboteur: Code Name — MoriTuri
PRODUCED BY AARON ROSENBERG
RELEASED THROUGH TWENTIETH CENTURY-FOX
Directed by Bernhard Wicki
Screenplay by Daniel Taradash

Robert Crain .... Marlon Brando
Captain Mueller .... Yul Brynner
Colonel Statter .... Trevor Howard
Dr. Ambach .... Wally Cox
Baldwin .... William Redfield
Esther .... Janet Margolin

1966

The Chase
PRODUCED BY SAM SPIEGEL
RELEASED THROUGH COLUMBIA PICTURES
Directed by Arthur Penn
Screenplay by Lillian Hellman

Calder	Marlon Brando
Anna	Jane Fonda
Bubber	Robert Redford
Val Rogers	E. G. Marshall
Ruby	Angie Dickinson
Emily Stewart	Janice Rule
Mrs. Briggs	Jocelyn Brando

The Appaloosa
PRODUCED BY ALAN MILLER
RELEASED THROUGH UNIVERSAL PICTURES
Directed by Sidney J. Furie
Screenplay by James Bridges and Roland Kibbee

Matt	Marlon Brando
Trini	Anjanette Comer
Chup	John Saxon
Squint-eye	Alex Montoya

1967

A Countess from Hong Kong
PRODUCED BY JEROME EPSTEIN
RELEASED THROUGH UNIVERSAL PICTURES
Directed by Charles Chaplin
Original screenplay by Charles Chaplin

Ogden	Marlon Brando
Natascha	Sophia Loren
Harvey	Sydney Chaplin
Marta	Tippi Hedren
Miss Gaulswallow	Margaret Rutherford
Old Steward	Charles Chaplin

Reflections in a Golden Eye
PRODUCED BY RAY STARK
WARNER BROTHERS-SEVEN ARTS
Directed by John Huston
Screenplay by Chapman Mortimer and Gladys Hill

Major Weldon Penderton	Marlon Brando
Leonora Penderton	Elizabeth Taylor
Lt. Col. Morris Langdon	Brian Keith
Alison Langdon	Julie Harris

1968

Candy
PRODUCED BY ROBERT HAGGIAG WITH SELIG J. SELIGMAN AND
  PETER ZOREF, EXECUTIVE PRODUCERS
RELEASED THROUGH CINERAMA RELEASING CORP.
Directed by Christian Marquand
Screenplay by Buck Henry

Grindl	Marlon Brando
Candy	Ewa Aulin
The Hunchback	Charles Aznavour
McPhisto	Richard Burton
Dr. Krankeit	James Coburn
Dr. Dunlap	John Huston
General Smight	Walter Matthau
Emmanuel	Ringo Starr

1969

The Night of the Following Day
PRODUCED BY HUBERT CORNFIELD FOR JERRY GERSHWIN-
  ELLIOT KASTNER PRODUCTION UNIT OF GINA FILMS
RELEASED THROUGH UNIVERSAL STUDIOS
Directed by Hubert Cornfield
Screenplay by Hubert Cornfield

Chauffeur	Marlon Brando
Lear	Richard Boone
The Blonde	Rita Moreno
Girl	Pamela Franklin
Friendly	Jess Hahn

1970

Burn! (Queimada)
PRODUCED BY ALBERTO GRIMALDI
RELEASED BY UNITED ARTISTS
Directed by Gillo Pontecorvo
Original screenplay by Gilo Pontecorvo, Franco Salinas,
and Giorgio Artorio

Sir William Walker	Marlon Brando
Jose Dolores	Evaristo Marquez
Teddy Sanchez	Renato Salvatori
Shelton	Norman Hill
General Prada	Tom Lyons

1971

The Nightcomers
PRODUCED BY MICHAEL WINNER FOR ELLIOTT KRASNER–J. KAN-
TER–ALAN LADD, JR.–SCIMITAR PRODUCTIONS
RELEASED THROUGH AVCO-EMBASSY
Directed by Michael Winner
Original screenplay by Michael Hastings

Peter Quint	Marlon Brando
Miss Jessel	Stephanie Beacham
Flora	Verna Harvey
Miles	Christopher Ellis

1972

The Godfather
PRODUCED BY AL RUDDY
PARAMOUNT PICTURES
Directed by Francis Ford Coppola
Screenplay by Mario Puzo and Francis Ford Coppola

The Godfather(Don Vito Corleone). Marlon Brando
Michael Corleone .... Al Pacino
Sonny Corleone ....James Caan
Fredo Corleone .... John Cazale
Tom Hagen .... Robert Duval
McCluskey .... Sterling Hayden
Barzini .... Richard Conte
Johnny Fontane .... Al Martino
Mama Corleone ....Morgana King
Jack Woltz ....John Marley
Kay Adams .... Dianne Keaton
Apollonia ....Simonetta Stefanelli
Luca Brasi .... Lenny Montana
Clemenenza .... Richard Castellano

(Projected for 1973 release)

Last Tango in Paris
Directed by Bernardo Bertolucci
Original screenplay by Bernardo Bertolucci and
  Franco Arcalli

1 2 3 4 5 6 7 ← P Y → 9 8 7 6 5 4 3